Translation of

A City and the Dead;
Zablotow Alive and Destroyed
-
Memorial Book of Zabolotov

Translation of

Ir u-metim; Zablotow ha-melea ve-ha-hareva

Original Yizkor Book Edited by Former Residents of Zablotow in Israel and the USA

Published in Tel-Aviv Israel, 1949

Published by JewishGen

An Affiliate of the Museum of Jewish Heritage - A Living Memorial to the Holocaust
New York

A City and the Dead; Zablotow Alive and Destroyed
Memorial Book of Zabolotov

First Printing: January 2017, Tevet 5777
Second Printing: March 2019, Adar II 5779

Translator: Schmuel Kahati
Translation Project Coordinator: Ronald B. Schechter
Layout: Joel Alpert
Cover Design: Nili Goldman

Published by JewishGen, Inc.
An Affiliate of the Museum of Jewish Heritage
A Living Memorial to the Holocaust
36 Battery Place, New York, NY 10280

The mission of the JewishGen organization is to produce a translation of the original work and we cannot verify the accuracy of statements or alter facts cited.

Printed in the United States of America by Lightning Source, Inc.

Library of Congress Control Number (LCCN): 2016954355

ISBN: 978-1-939561-44-2 (hard cover: 172 pages, alk. paper)

Cover photograph: Photograph of Thau Sperber, Dina with her son Bronislaw, 1928, Courtesy of Yad Vashem.

Back Cover Credit: From a post card labeled "Zablotow. Rynek – Ringplats."

iv

JewishGen and the Yizkor-Books-in-Print Project

This book has been published by the **Yizkor-Books-in-Print Project,** as part of the **Yizkor Book Project** of **JewishGen, Inc.**

JewishGen, Inc. is a non-profit organization founded in 1987 as a resource for Jewish genealogy. Its website [www.jewishgen.org] serves as an international clearinghouse and resource center to assist individuals who are researching the history of their Jewish families and the places where they lived. JewishGen provides databases, facilitates discussion groups, and coordinates projects relating to Jewish genealogy and the history of the Jewish people. In 2003, JewishGen became an affiliate of the **Museum of Jewish Heritage - A Living Memorial to the Holocaust** in New York.

The **JewishGen Yizkor Book Project** was organized to make more widely known the existence of Yizkor (Memorial) Books written by survivors and former residents of various Jewish communities throughout the world. Later, volunteers connected to the different destroyed communities began cooperating to have these books translated from the original language—usually Hebrew or Yiddish—into English, thus enabling a wider audience to have access to the valuable information contained within them. As each chapter of these books was translated, it was posted on the JewishGen website and made available to the general public.

The **Yizkor-Books-in-Print Project** began in 2011 as an initiative to print and publish Yizkor Books that had been fully translated, so that hard copies would be available for purchase by the descendants of these communities and also by scholars, universities, synagogues, libraries, and museums.

These Yizkor books have been produced almost entirely through the volunteer effort of researchers from around the world, assisted by donations from private individuals. The books are printed and sold at near cost, so as to make them as affordable as possible. Our goal is to make this important genre of Jewish literature and history available in English in book form, so that people can have the personal histories of their ancestral towns on their bookshelves for themselves and for their children and grandchildren.

A list of all published translated Yizkor Books in the project with prices and ordering information can be found at:
http://www.jewishgen.org/Yizkor/ybip.html

Lance Ackerfeld, Yizkor Book Project Manager

Joel Alpert, Yizkor-Book-in-Print Project Coordinator

JewishGen
Yizkor Book Project

This book is presented by the
Yizkor Books in Print Project
Project Coordinator: Joel Alpert

Part of the
Yizkor Books Project of JewishGen, Inc.
Project Manager: Lance Ackerfeld

These books have been produced solely through volunteer effort
of individuals from around the world. The books are printed and
sold at near cost, so as to make them as affordable as possible.

Our goal is to make this history and important genre of Jewish
literature available in English in book form so that people can have
the near-personal histories of their ancestral towns on their bookshelves for themselves and for their children and grandchildren.

Any donations to the Yizkor Books Project are appreciated.

Please send donations to:
Yizkor Book Project
JewishGen
36 Battery Place
New York, NY 10280

JewishGen, Inc. is an affiliate of the
Museum of Jewish Heritage
A Living Memorial to the Holocaust

Translation of

A City and the Dead;
Zablotow Alive and Destroyed
-
Memorial Book of Zabolotov (Zablotow)
(Zabolotiv, Ukraine)
48°28' / 25°18'

Translation of

Ir u-metim; Zablotow ha-melea ve-ha-hareva

Original Yizkor Book Edited by Former Residents of Zablotow in Israel and the USA

Published in Tel-Aviv Israel, 1949

This is a translation from: *Ir u-metim; Zablotow ha-melea ve-ha-hareva*
A City and the Dead; Zablotow Alive and Destroyed
Published in Tel Aviv by the Former Residents of Zablotow in Israel and the USA
1949 (in Hebrew and Yiddish), 218 pages

Dedication for this Translation

In Memory of Ron Schechter's ancestors who came from Zablotow: Grandparents Sam and Gussie Schechter immigrated in early 1900s; Great grandparents Hershe Wolf and Taube Schechter; Great-great grandparents Scheye and Ruchel Schechter; and grandmother's parents Hashe Liebe an Schendel Tauber, who were all from Zablotow and the grandmother's sisters and grandfather's cousins who perished in the Holocaust.

MAP OF UKRAINE IN 2014

Map showing Zablotov in the Ukraine

Farms and Villages which were part of the town

Il'intse
Oleshkov
Areletse
Gan'kovtsy
Voysekhovitse
Dzhurov
Chalibitchin

Tulukow
Trachi (Trojca)
Troschinich (Druzhinets)
Roznov
Rudniki

Geopolitical Information:

Zabolotiv, Ukraine: <u>48°28' N, 25°17' E</u>
12 miles ESE of Kolomyya, 13 miles W of Snyatyn.

Alternate names for the town are: Zabolotiv [Ukrainian], Zabłotów [Polish], Zablutov [Yiddish], Zabolotov [Russian], Zablatov, Zablotov, Zablotuv, Zabolotyiv

	Town	District	Province	Country	
Before WWI (c. 1900):	Zabłotów	Śniatyn	Galicia	Austrian Empire	
Between the wars (c. 1930):	Zabłotów	Śniatyn	Stanisławów	Poland	
After WWII (c. 1950):	Zabolotov			Soviet Union	
Today (c. 2000):	Zabolotiv			Ukraine	

Jewish Population in 1890: 2009

Notes: Ukrainian: Заболотів. Yiddish: זאַבלאָטאָוו Russian: Заболотов. Hebrew: זבולוטוב

<u>Nearby Jewish Communities</u>:

Demiche 1 miles E
Dzhurov 5 miles SSE
Rozhniv 7 miles SSW
Banyliv 8 miles SSE
Hvizdets 8 miles N
Knyazhe 9 miles ESE
Miliye 9 miles S
Vilyavche 10 miles SSE
Dzhurkov 12 miles NNW
Vashkivtsi 12 miles ESE
Kolomyya 12 miles WNW
Snyatyn 13 miles E
Kosiv 13 miles SW
Pystan 13 miles WSW
Moskalivka 14 miles SW

Kuty 16 miles SSW
Vyzhnytsya 16 miles SSW
Yaseniv-Pilnyy 16 miles NE
Chernyatyn 16 miles NNE
Yabluniv 16 miles WSW
Chortovets 16 miles N
Nyzhni Stanivitzi 17 miles SE
Obertyn 17 miles NNW
Horodenka 17 miles NE
Nepolokivtsi 17 miles ESE
Vyzhenka 18 miles SSW
Pechenizhyn 19 miles W
Davydivtsi 19 miles E
Kostintsy 19 miles SE
Berehomet 20 miles

Notes to the Reader:

Within the text the reader will note "{34}" standing ahead of a paragraph. This indicates that the material translated below was on page 34 of the original book. However, when a paragraph was split between two pages in the original book, the marker is placed in this book after the end of the paragraph for ease of reading.

Also please note that all references within the text of the book to page numbers, refer to the page numbers of the original Yizkor Book.

The original book can be seen online at the NY Public Library site:

http://yizkor.nypl.org/index.php?id=1232

In order to obtain a list of all Shoah victims from Zablotov, the reader should access the Yad Vashem web site listed below; one can also search for specific family names using family name option. These lists are continually updated by Yad Vashem, so it is worthwhile to periodically search these lists.

There is much valuable information available on this web site, including the Pages of Testimony, etc.

http://yvng.yadvashem.org

A list of this book and all books available in the Yizkor-Book-In-Print Project along with prices is available at:
                    http://www.jewishgen.org/Yizkor/ybip.html

Title Page of Original Yizkor Book

עִיר וּמֵתִים

זַבְּלוֹטוֹב הַמְּלֵאָה וְהֶחָרֵבָה

צו מַצֵבָה, דֶר ניכטע „קְרָנְצי" וואטרמן,
גדנק־ספר, צוהיטט קינדער, וו יִיב־מַאן.
געגבן דורך אנקל אברהם הכהן קיץ.

תל־אביב אים חודש מרחשון יאר תשי'.

יוצא לאור על־ידי יוצאי זבלוטוב בארק־ישראל ובאמריקה

1949   תל־אביב   תש'ט

Translation of the Title Page of Original Yiddish Book

Town and People

The complete and the Ruined Zablotov

A present for niece, "Krantzi" Waserman,
Memorial book, slaughter of children, wife and man.
Presented by uncle Avraham HaKohen Kish.

TEL AVIV, Marcheshvan 5710.   [November 1949]

Published by the former residents of Zablotow, in Israel and The United States

1949   Tel-Aviv   5709

Table of Contents

Notes

Introduction

The former residents of our town meet in Tel-Aviv during Chanukah of 1946 on the forth anniversary of the first "action" that took place in Zablotow. It was decided to publish a compilation, which would include the events in our birthplace Zablotow, until its bitter end. The former residents of our town now living in the United States, agreed to the decision and assisted greatly in the funding of the publication.

The carrying out of the task was handed over to Mr. Meir Hanish and Mr. G. Karsel who are now presenting it to the public.

The obstacles and delays on the road to success were many. Many who were approached had refused, including some that had previously promised to help. This was compounded by the war and by the troubles of the publishers, who were unable to devote all their time to the book.

It is certain that some inaccuracies have been included in the history of our town, and flaws exist in important areas, but unfortunately, we had no reliable historical source about our city's distant past, other then the notes of Mr. Avraham Keish, which will enable the fulfillment of the task.

This book is published both in Hebrew and Yiddish in accordance with the wishes of the former residents of our city now living in the United States. They showed a great interest in this project, among them R' Yissachar Toy *Z"L*, who passed way during the preparation stages and did not live to see its conclusion, and R' Zeindel Sheinhorn.

We did not live to erect a monument for our city while most of her sons were alive, and when it was partially done, it was only after they were eliminated by the oppressor. May this book serve as a Memorial to all the righteous of Zablotow, who were mentioned or not mentioned here, and who were a link in the long chain of its history.

Preface

Written by Mr. G. Karsel

It is the privilege of our destroyed city to have this one and only special man, who is a tremendous source of personal knowledge of our city's history and its residents over the past 150 years - he is R' Avraham Keish, the author of our book.

He is the oldest survivor of our town, not only in a physical sense, but also, most importantly, is his wisdom. What is most important to the rescue of the history of our town, is his phenomenal ability to recall the names of many families and their descendants, now scattered all over the world. He did his best to revive the hundreds of characters of the town as though you were strolling down the streets of Zablotow, entering every home, recalling the previous owners who have changed through the generations, mixed in with various minor and major events, which left a deep impression.

You will probably notice how wide and encompassing the memory of our source is. All citizens are loved and cherished by him, as he casts deep love over them while describing what was destroyed, and the lively Jewish folklore which was cut off by the wicked.

It goes without saying that not every thing is remembered here. We, including the author R' Avraham Keish, did not imagine that Zablotow would be erased off the face of the earth, and we did not provide details of the past to future generations. Only while working on this publication, was the author able to describe some of the characters of the city. Even though this happened by chance, and after many years away from Zablotow, did he succeed in reviving the memory of previous generations, till the turn of the twentieth century. Should a mistake be found, it must be remembered that what we have here are the ashes saved from a burning fire. Our generation should be able to create and weave the continuation of these memories for him or for future generations.

The foundations were laid down by R' Avraham Keish in these beautiful memoirs. Just as he did not leave out anything in his memory that had happened in Zablotow, he did not bother noting biographical details about himself.

The first account of R' Avraham Keish as seen by a Zablotow youth is fascinating. During the first years after World War II, we are at the end of the old era, entering the yet unknown new world and into the Revival movement and Nationality. Streets are still rumbling after the Balfour Declaration and its ratification in San Remo, when a young boy stumbles into the Town's Beit Midrash, which is full to capacity, while the entire crowd is listening to a speaker on the podium. Standing there was an old Jewish figure, long beard down his chest, preaching vigorously for the settlement of Eretz Yisrael, quoting fluently by heart from our sages, and astonishingly enough also from our poet Chaim Nachman Bialik. Moreover, the speaker is not a "Zionist" preacher, but rather an influential Jewish merchant, a religious Chasid, known in this area. That was how R' Avraham Keish was seen by the author of this Preface.

That time he was no longer a resident of Zablotow, but Zablotow fondly remembered its son, still a young boy, excelling both in Torah and in Zionist involvement, at a time when it was still considered heresy, and was forbidden.

Born on Monday, second of Eyar 5626 (1866), he studied with the best teachers of Zablotow, among them R' Efrayim Fond and later R' Moshe Karsel and R' Menachem Mher. The latter were involved in a very high level of studies after becoming impoverished, and had a great impact on him. While R' Moshe Karsel directed him towards Torah studies, R' Menachem Mher knew how to open an aperture towards General Education. He did not restrain his students from studying writing and grammar and "foreign" knowledge (his own son, Zev Mher, published a "Story and Picture" book in Vienna in 5686 (1922). Following his General Education he secretly studied bookkeeping by correspondence, and supported himself after his marriage doing bookkeeping for wood-mills from around Galicia and Bukovina. Later he became rich and was one of the influential wood merchants of Galicia with businesses out of the country.

Thus, R' Avraham Keish the merchant, during the nineties of the last century was one of the first who dedicated himself full heartily to the Zionist National Idea. He was active in "Ahavat Zion" in Tarnow, one of the main assistants of R' Feivel Shreir and Dr. Abraham Salts - leaders of the community, from the first who joined Hertzl's movement and persuaded merchants and Chasidim, "Mizrachi" activist. For a while he was President of the "Mizrachi" in Stanislavov, planning all his life to settle in Eretz-Yisrael till he did so in 5684 (1924) when he immigrated to Eretz-Yisrael and settled there.

Here he deals in lumber, pioneering the development of this industry in Tel-Aviv into a large-scale operation with connections abroad. At the same time, not neglecting his public activities especially for the "Mizrachi", while Torah and studies (including Modern Hebrew literature and especially poetry) remain his favorites, and he always carried a book with him.

During later years, while his family was destroyed abroad, he left the lumber business and concentrated diligently on projects related to the ruined city of Zablotow and the remaining immigrants from there. Like a youngster full of vigor he concentrated on uniting the former residents of our town, and also bestowed his glow on us at each meeting and every gathering. In his calm and collected manner he entered our hearts and even among our brothers in the United State he became influential and well accepted and respected. This compilation would not have become a reality if not for his constant urging, his willingness to go and give a helping hand at any time and anywhere required. Whenever he was seen walking down the streets of Tel-Aviv, he represented the symbolic and collective image of our town with the goodness and superiority of its previous generations - our community, now destroyed.

Figure 1 - General view of Zablotow. The City Square and the street leading to the train station

Figure 2 - General view of Zablotow. The suburb of Demycze and the bridge.

In the City Streets

By Avraham Keish

I. Rabbis

Zablotow Rabbis

1. The first Rabbi of Zablotow, and the first of the Hager dynasty was R' David (Dudke) the son of the righteous rabbi R' Menachem Mendel from Kosov, the founder of the Hager dynasty of Rabbis in Galicia, Bukovina and more, and the author of "Ahavat Shalom" (Love of Peace). R' David also wrote a book titled " Tzemach David" (Plant of David).

R' David's wife was Pessi-Leah, the only daughter of the famous righteous rabbi R' Moshe Leib from Sasov. The Chasidim explained that the Rabbi called his daughter Pessi-Leah because of the clue embedded in the initials of her name. P"L stands (in Hebrew) for "future Passover", namely, in accordance to our sages who say: In the month of Nissan Bnei Yisrael were freed and during that month they will be redeemed. And they add: The righteous R' Meir'el from Przemyshel was for a while the student of The righteous R' Moshe Leib from Sasov. When the housekeeper was not at home, the student R' Meir'el put the baby Pessi-Leah to sleep and sang to her soft quiet lullabies. Later, after she left home, he used to ask about her from people who came to him from Zablotow for blessings and sent her his regards.

R' David and his wife Pessi-Leah were well known for their generosity and hospitality. People flocked there daily to receive their blessings, men women and children by the thousands from Zablotow, the surrounding areas and from far away places who asked for salvation and healing. Some waited days for their turn. They enjoyed economic success, money was pouring in, but they spread it as quickly through generous donations to the poor near and far and various organization so, by the end of each day there was nothing left. They themselves had to buy on credit at the local stores, and Shabbos necessities were paid only on the following week. R' David had a lot of influence on his Chasidim by his manners, actions, love of Torah and for his fellow Jews. After his death, Pessi inherited his position, she received notes (Tsetelachs), and blessed people and so the Chasidim continued to stream in as they had before when R' David was alive.

R' David and Pessi were blessed with four sons and two daughter. The eldest was R' Yakov (Yankele), the second R' Menachem (Mendel), the third R' Tzvi (Hershle), the fourth R' Michael (Mechle). One daughter was the wife of R' Itzele from Bohosh - Romania, the second was the wife of the famous R' David, who wrote the book "Minchat Chinuch ". R' David and Pessi died and were buried in Zablotow.

2. The second rabbi of Zablotow was R' David's eldest son, R' Yankele (Yakov). He was a nice looking man with a full beard down his chest. He excelled in his conversations with the people and his teaching, people came to him, as they did to his parents, for blessings, remedies, and even emulates. Dan Fisher from Lukavets in Bukovina, one of his admirers, gave him a special gift - a carriage with two white and very expensive horses. It was said that he received this gift after his blessing successfully caused his barren wife to become pregnant. R' Yakov used this carriage in his many excursions out of town visiting his Chasidim. They were very happy when he visited them on Thursdays staying over Shabbos till the following Thursday. His followers used to welcome him a few miles before he reached the town, and escorted him into town holding torches, running along side his carriage and yelling "The Rabbi is entering our town". People came in from all the neighboring villages, and when he entered the Synagogue which was filled to capacity, they all stood up. People were happy and joyous all week when the Rabbi stayed in town, but for Shabbos dinner tables were set-up with a variety of dishes especially Kugels, wine and whiskey. Everybody was in a good mood, they start out singing then dance. Tzetelachs (notes) and donations were in abundance. The Kosov's Rabbis also participated in the festivities when they were in town.

2.1 The third Rabbi of Zablotow was R' Menachem (Mendele), the only son of R' Yakov. After his father's death he inherited his father's position. His wife was Nichele, they had five sons and three daughter. The eldest, R' Davidel, married the daughter of a rich estate-owner from Vasel'kovtsy in the Tarnopol District. It was a very large estate with fields, forests and a large farm which he inherited after the death of his father-in-law. He was a very successful farmer and became very rich, but did not forget his origins, acting as befitting a Rabbi's Grand-son, he fulfilled the Mitzva of hospitality, he supported his father and brothers and was well known for his charity and donations.

2.2 The fourth rabbi of Zablotow was R' Moshe the second son of R' Mendele, who inherited the position after his father's death. The third son, R' Isaac, married the daughter of a rich Jewish man from Bratishev, and lived in his house. The fourth son, R' Yossi, married the daughter of the Rabbi of Tysmenitsa, inheriting the position after his death. The fifth son, R' Gershon, was a great scholar becoming a Rabbi in Touste where they loved him for his great knowledge. His daughter Hindele, married R'

Israel Berger of Probezhna in Galicia he was a great scholar and speaker, and wrote a book. His son, R' Moshe Berger, lived in Stanislav. R' Menachem's second daughter, married R' Chaim Wallfram's son, an ordinary Jewish merchant.

During the period of the first Rabeim, including R' Mendele, Jews enjoyed the good life. Many came from the outlying communities filling up the hotels, restaurants and stores. Gabaim, assistants, servants and their families too, benefited from the situation. Their house, standing in the town center, was a source of joy, happiness and songs especially on holidays. The Gabaim working in the community, added their contribution to the happy environment.

As mentioned above, the fourth rabbi of Zablotow was R' Moshe the second son of R' Menachem. His wife Elisheva (Shevale) who survived him, was a smart woman. They brought-up their two sons, R' Chaim and R' David, in the Jewish way of Torah and Mitzvos. A new law requiring Rabbis to be fluent in two languages - Polish and Ukrainian - they have learnt these languages with a private teacher. R' Moshe did not live long, he was replaced by his eldest son R' Chaim who escaped to Vienna during the War then returned home to Zablotow a few years after the end of the First World War.

2.3 The fifth and last Rabbi of Zablotow was R' Chaim, a great scholar who sat and learned Torah all day . His wife, Reizel, an educated woman, efficiently managed the house-work with her mother-in-law. They and all citizens of Zablotow, were killed by the Nazis in 1942.

The first four Rabbis who concentrated mainly on heavenly worship, did not have the time to guide people in Jewish Law and be Jewish judges. Each one selected a Dayan (a Jewish Judge) who held court and passed sentence, decided what was allowed or disallowed, performed marriages and divorces, etc. He sat in the Rabbi's synagogue which included a large hall, a women section and the Rabbis house. Most of the important citizens used to pray in that synagogue and there they held the Shabbos "Tisch". It also served as a meeting place for the young boys before they were tested for the army. For three months they stayed awake at night drinking and singing in-order to prepare themselves for the army test.

Demycze Rabbis

Demycze was a suburb of Zablotow. It was considered a separate municipal entity, but was part of Zablotow's Jewish community.

The first Rabbi there was R' Mendele, the second son of R' Dudke, who was the first Rabbi of Zablotow. He built a very large synagogue with a large woman's section. It was called "Viznica Synagogue" due to the large number of Viznica Chasidim there. He had only a few Chasidim but they provided him with enough income with their Tsetalachs and donations. He had one daughter, Gittle, who married R' Yoseph David from Russia who was popular in the community, a scholar, a Chazan with beautiful melodies for the High Holiday prayers and he was destined for the Rabbi position. Unfortunately he passed away at a young age.

Figure 3 - A group of citizens: R' Avraham Hager Rabbi of Demycze, is in the middle, R' Mordechai Ashkenazi, at his side, R' Shmayah Salpeter, on the other side

The position was filled by R' Mendele's grandson, R' Avraham. Although he was called the Rabbi of Demycze he realized he must have followers in Zablotow too and he tried to be the Rabbi of both communities. With the help of an acquaintance he acquired a certificate from the manager of Sniatin District which ratified him as the Rabbi of Zablotow. (Until that time no Rabbi had obtained that kind of certificate). This caused a great rift between him and his cousin (second cousin), R'

Moshe and his son R' Chaim who where the Rabbis in Zablotow at that time. It developed into an open split between the two Jewish communities of Zablotow and Demycze, until the authority awarded both of them ratification.

R' Avraham, like his grandfather R' Mendele, established a Dayan position in Demycze who assisted him. He sat in the Viznica house, and in later years moved to R' Avraham's house, when he moved to Zablotow. R' Avraham's father in-law was R' Mordechai Ashkenazi, the son of the Dayan of Kalush in Galicia. He knew how to learn and had a teaching certificate. He became the Dayan of Demycze after the death of the first Dayan, and hoped to be the next Rabbi, however they all perished in 1942. During Chanukah of 1942 when the first Action took place in Zablotow, R' Avraham Hager and his family marched in the first row to their slaughter. He actually found a hiding place but when he realized that the people were being led away, he got out and joined them at the killing ground. His brother, R' Itche who served as a rabbi in nearby Roznov, miraculously made his way during the war to Eretz-Israel. He lives in Jerusalem.

R' Avraham obtained from the authorities in Sniatin a permit to register all births, deaths and marriages in Zablotow and the surroundings. This was an official position, with a fixed income from each registry and from providing copies. It brought him honor and respect. It was given only to those who were considered "clean" and he had to learn Polish and Ukrainian. He was the last one to hold that position when he was killed in Chanukah of 1942. The first one to hold that position was the Mayor of Zablotow, R' Meir Rata, he passed it on to his son R' Tzvi and then it was passed on to his grandson R' Fishel. Others who held that positions were R' Moshe Sheinhoren and R' Chaim Zimmel Singer who was the mayor for a short time. Great fights broke out between those vying for the position, forcing foreign intervention.

Petashnitzin Rabbis

R' Dudke's third son, R' Tzvi Hershele, settled in Petashnitzin, a small town near Kolomyja. He built a large house and synagogue in the center of town. He was accepted with great honor and was chosen Rabbi, and made his livelihood from his large followers and Chasidim.

His only son, R' Gershon, was well versed in worldly matters as well as Jewish studies. He married the daughter of a rich man and joined him in his business of trade in lumber, forest industries, and even in oil fields. (which exist in abundance around Petashnitzin and Sloboda. His sons and daughters received a Jewish education in the spirit of his Jewish ancestry, as well as some general knowledge befitting the spirit of those times. He inherited his father's position after his death with the agreement of most of the citizens and served the community without pay. He belonged to those who gave of themselves and did not accepted anything in return.

He married off his daughter (or his grand-daughter), to R' Yakov the son of R' Alter Salpeter, a well known wealthy man from Sloboda-Rongurska, who had a large house and owned a general goods store and many other properties and land in town. During that time English and French experts started coming to the area in-order to develop oil and wax drilling. R' Alter gave his land in Sloboda to one of these companies for 50% of the expected future profits. It proved to be a success. They struck oil and wealth. From that time on his house was opened to the poor where they received food and shelter and many gifts. R' Alter was a great admirer of R' Mendele from Viznica. It is rumored that each quarter of a year he donated to the Rabbi 500 Rubel, which was a great sum in those days. Some say that he donated a similar sum monthly to the Rabbi whom he considered to be his partner in the oil fields. However, mother nature's gift did not last forever. After twenty profuse years production started to dwindle until it stopped all together. Those few who kept their riches did not suffer, but most became impoverished and the town and its surroundings shamefully lost their glory. R' Alter who used to spread, waste and share his wealth, was left empty-handed. His son, R' Yakov, was forced to sell almost for nothing, the house and land which were valued at a half a million Rubbels. After the death of R' Alter, R' Yakov moved to Kolomyja and was a small lumber dealer.

Storozhinets Rabbis

R' Dudke's fourth and youngest son, R' Mechel, chose to settle in Storozhinets. His wife was the daughter of the righteous R' Eliezer the son of the famous R' Shalom Rokach from Belz. He built a large house and synagogue, was accepted with great honor and made his livelihood from his large followers and Chasidim. His sons and sons-in-law became famous rabbis well accepted by their communities.

His son Shalom was Rabbi in Mald Banila in Bukovina, and found his way to London England during the war. His first son-in-law, R' Mordechai Tabak, who married his daughter Malkale, belonged to a noble family and was a great scholar and Chazan. They found their livelihood by selling wine and she worked in the local grocery store. Their sons were brought up to follow Torah, worship God and given some general knowledge.

His second son-in-law, the famous R' David, was the rabbi of Kiydantse in Bukovina for a few years. Their sons were brought up to follow the Torah, worship God and given general knowledge. His son was R' Menachem Hager who was for a while the Dayan in Halitcz in Galicia, then in Neistat. He was one of the original activists of "The Mizrachi" movement who not only preached, but also followed it with many activities. He was elected as Chairman of the Mizrachi in Lwow, and moved to Lwow to serve in the Mizrachi Directorate of Galicia. He was the man behind the "MTT" (which stands for Torah from Zion) charity organization in Lwow, which supported Jewish religious schools in Galicia. He had traveled to the United States to raise funds for the organization, and was very successful. Finally he was elected Rabbi of Sosnovitch. There too he excelled in his Zionist activities to the dismay of the Belz Rabbi. He was captured by the Russians but managed to emigrate with his family to Eretz-Israel. He is active here in Tel-Aviv at the Mizrachi National Headquarters, and serves as Chairman of the Chevra-Kadisha of Tel-Aviv.

Gabaeim of Zablotow

The first Gabay of Zablotow was R' Levi Salpeter, a tall man with a long white beard across his chest. He was a learned man with meticulously clean clothes. He served R' Dudke (the first Rabbi) and, for a short time, R' Yakov too. He excelled in telling stories about Chasidim with grace and charm. Blessed be he who heard his stories. His son, Shlomo, served R' Mendele in Demycze all his life and was very much like his father. His son, R' Eliezer, was a great singer enliven the "Tisch" (feast) at the Rabbi's house. Later he left Zablotow and immigrated to the United States with his sisters.

R' Elimelech, nick-named "King Solomon" followed R' Levi as a Gabay in Zablotow. He was well read and even had a bit of "general" knowledge. He was very good looking told jokes and had a wide smile. He spoke a few languages fluently and was considered a reincarnation of Hershele from Ostropoly who was born solely for entertaining and making people happy. He wore his famous Purim mask while reading the Megilah in Ukrainian, he read Akdamuth on Shavuot in Ukrainian too changing the contents and version as he went along. He was greatly skilled at reading aloud making people enjoy his stories very much. Another crowd pleaser was R' Menachem Mendel Butschki (Was it his family name or his nickname, it is not known), maybe he was a Gabay or maybe just a another Chasid from the crowd. He arrived every Holiday to perform and rejoice with the Chasidim bringing different songs, prayers and melodies for each holiday. On Simchat Torah he got up on the roof attic, built to be the highest in town, (like the Temple in Jerusalem). He sat out on the roof wrapped in a white Kitle (garment), wearing a Shtreimel (wide fur hat) sipping whisky. Kids surrounded the house and he sang songs, melodies and High-Holiday prayers. He yelled: " What day is it today? Shimchat Torah?" with the kids was answering gleefully. It was by itself a miracle that he stayed up there not slipping off the sloped roof and breaking his neck.

When "King Solomon" died, R' Menachem Mendel Butschki disappeared and the joyous atmosphere disappeared with him. The Rabbi's court turned dull and gloomy causing a real drop in income. A miserable one-horse buggy of a poor Jewish Carter replaced the carriage and two white horses. The Rabbi was still traveling to nearby towns and to far away cities and towns in other countries - Rumania and Bukovina - too, but this time for his livelihood. He used first or second class, and later even third class. Entering towns he was not, as in prior years, surrounded by torch holding crowds. They disappeared completely.

Shabbos "Tisch" was empty with "Kugel's and wines served only as tokens. The synagogue was not crowded even when the Rabbi himself was the prayer leader (Chazan). On weekdays and Saturday nights no Chasidim came over for blessings or Tzetalachs (notes). The innkeeper, himself a veteran Chasid, accompanied by an acquaintance loitered around town looking for donations for the Rabbi who was leaving town on Thursday.

II. Citizens (1790-1942)

R' Avraham Yehuda Leib Shfarber and his wife Etti. An intelligent man who rented a large farm, employed farm workers but was unsuccessful and lost a fortune. He purchased a saloon and became a Bartender in the village of Oleshkov. Here too he was busy more with his Torah studies then in his business, he treated many guests for free and got involved in community activities in Zablotow. In his old age he moved into his large house in Zablotow which was located in the city market, and had a restaurant for none Jews and worked as a Bartender alongside his wife and five daughters. They had two sons who were educated in the Jewish tradition. He belonged to Kosov's Chasidim, prayed in their synagogue, went daily to the Mikvah and was the first one in last one out of the Beit Midrash. Although not a wealthy man he always supported charities and those who approached him.

His Daughter, **Chaiche**, married R' Natan a grandson of the Rabbi of Kuti who was a sincere God fearing and orthodox Jew. He feared being drafted to the army so he carried his wife's family name. She was a very capable woman who ran their store, however they had no children so they divorced after ten years of marriage as required by Jewish law, remarried and each had their own children.

His second daughter, **Leah**, was very modest and pious married R' Moshe Gross. They lived at his parents house for a while, then opened a store and eventually moved to Kolomyja. There he became successful in the lumber trade. They had a small house. Their son, Naftali, emigrated to the United States, excelled in literature and became a famous Yiddish writer and translated The Bible to Yiddish (he also published a few poetry books and contributed to a few periodical). The rest of his sons and his only daughter were educated in Torah and general knowledge.

His son, **R' David Shfarber** was fluent in German and Polish. He had excellent handwriting and a tremendous memory. He was a certified teacher . At the age of 19 he was drafted into the army despite being married at the time and the father of a baby girl. He served in Prague and was promoted. At the end of the compulsory three years he was persuaded to stay in the army and become an officer, but he refused and returned home to his family. Relations with his wife, Dreiza, were cool from the beginning, livelihood was scarce, so after a few years they divorced. Their daughter Esther, was a grown women at that time, educated and pretty.

He remarried Pessi, a young, educated, determined virgin, daughter of R' Zev Rosenboim. They had two girls and a boy. He had a hard time supporting his family, so he wandered all the way to Montreal in Canada, where he had a rich relative who assisted him. When he settled, after a few years he brought the family to Montreal, he became rich but did not forget his family and friends in Zablotow sending them large sums of money from time to time and also donated handsomely to the Rabbis of Zablotow and Kosov.

R' David was well respected in his community, famous for his generous heart and sat on many committees, was chairman of the UJA, a Justice of the Peace, and few charity organizations. Considering himself a veteran Zionist he dreamt of visiting Eretz-Israel one day. He fulfilled his dream in 1926 when he was 80 years old and sick. He crossed the entire country giving donations every-where; not a single institute in Yerushalayim or in Tel-Aviv that he did not visit and support. He stayed for two months spending most of the time with the poor. He yearned to settle in Eretz-Israel but his wife and children did not want to hear of it, kept asking him by a way of daily letters and Telegrams, to return home, settle his business and then move to Eretz-Israel - which he did not live to do. On his way back to Montreal he went through Zablotow and the Rabbi of Kosov.

One son and a daughter became specialist Doctors, another son (Marcus Shfarber) was a famous lawyer and a Member of Parliament where he was a great political speaker.

R' Natan, the second son of R' Avraham Yehuda Leib, loved reading, writing and languages. As a young boy he showed an inclination towards the arts, wood carving and painting. After completing Gemara and Bible studies he continued to work with an expert room-painter (It was a common custom in those days). He excelled and this turned to be his livelihood. He got married and with the help of his brother David moved to Canada and succeeded there too in his profession. He continued in his traditional Jewish ways, and supported his family, on occasion, but never left Canada.

A third daughter, **Branche,** married Moshe from the town of Petashnizin. After losing his money in trade he emigrated to the United States where he lived comfortably as a trader.

The youngest daughter, **Freima**, married R' David Aryeh Hager, a grandson of the famous R' Levi Yitzchak from Berdichev.

He became an orphan at a young age, and his relative the righteous Rabbi Yakov Shimshon Hager from Kosov, took him into his home and considered him his son. He was brought up together with the Rabbi's only son, R' Moshele, and they became inseparable. R' Yakov Shimshon married him off with Gitle, the eldest daughter of his good friend and a rich man, R' Moshe Shfarber who owned a large farm and was considered one of the wealthiest. R' Moshe rented a large farm in Ilinitz for the young couple, where they were very successful and R' David Aryeh managed the farm and the books. However, Gitle was barren, they divorced and he left her on the farm.

He married Friema as mentioned above, and after the death of R' Avraham Yehuda Leib he inherited the house and the restaurant. During the First World War the whole family moved to Vienna, where he died shortly after. Their children including their only son, Avraham Zeide emigrated to the United States, and later brought their mother over, too. One daughter was married to R' Natan Keish, who was one of the founders of "Poalei Zion" in Stanislav.

R' Avraham Yakov Fuchs. A humble old Jewish bartender. Feibish Fuchs, his son, was a small-built, small-time merchant who enjoyed learning. Every Shabbos afternoon he joined R' Aaron Keish to hear Torah from the 'source'. His sons, Menachem and Yitzchak Fuchs went house to house as private teachers.

His son-in-law Yakov Fishkis was an egg dealer. His son-in-law Fishel owned a one-horse carriage in which he shuttled passengers to Kolomyja for a quarter of the price of the train. He was also the intermediary between a local storekeeper and his supplier from Kolomyja. Another son died young but he had two boys, Eliezer and Aaron (Orche) Fuchs. They both owned a carriage and continued shuttling merchandise to and from Kolomyja. Aaron later immigrated to the United States and it is rumored he left Judaism and became a gangster.

R' Avraham (Avremel) Toy. A tall man, a landowner, had a large house and a barn next to the train station. He had a few children who were educated in Cheder and farming. R' Leib Toy, his son, married Chaike, the daughter of R' Tzvi (Rubin) and they both left Zablotow and emigrated to the United States.

R' Avraham (the son of Menche) was a Gemara and bible Teacher. He was a sickly man and died young. His brother Fishel was an economist working for a landowner. A second brother, Netta, inherited their mother's small house and had a small pottery shop. He used to display his wares on the sidewalk in-front of the shop, where passersby often tripped over them, causing commotion and fights. Netta's son-in-law, R' Avraham Laker was his heir. He was from Putila, became a Chasid of the Demycze's Rabbi and brought up his children with a proper Jewish education.

R' Avraham Chelm had a house across from the synagogue with a carpentry workshop, and a shed for his son's horse and carriage.

R' Avraham Leib Chamdrool, a simple Jew had a house across from R' Yehoshua Miller and later moved across the Jail. He was a small time pottery dealer and augmented his income as a beggar. He also used to help himself to meals at community festive dinners. He trained his children in pottery and a bit of Jewish education. His Brother-in-law (or other relation), R' Yisrael Kovale, lived with them.

R' Avraham Karmes was a merchant and had a small house. He provided his children with a proper Jewish education.

R' Avraham Hager, an honest man produced Honey at his home. Nisan and Hainich Hager, his sons, were educated to live as proper God worshipping Jews.

R' Alter (Leibel) Greif was a scholar, worked as a bartender and inherited a large house in Demycze. Every Shabbos he gave a lecture in the old Beit Hamidrash on the weekly portion of the Torah. He was a wonderful interpreter and 30-40 people attended the lecture which started at three PM and lasted two hours. He never missed a lecture despite the long walk from Demycze. His student loved him and gave him great honor. R' Yitzchak Greif, his eldest son, had a large house and a brick factory out of town. R' Yakov Greif, his son-in-law, was a well respected scholar and owned a large warehouse for lumber and roofing material. R' Chaim Greif, his second son, was a merchant and owned a house. R' David Greif, his third son, was a great scholar, continues his Jewish studies, became an expert in Jewish Law and accepted the position of a Rabbi somewhere in Galicia.

R' Alter Perel's, a great scholar was first a merchant then later when he lost his money became a very successful teacher. Tzvi Perel's, his son, inherited his father's tradition.

R' Alter (Yehuda Moshe) Teicher was an honest and quiet Jew whose occupation was bartending and an artist. Used to give a lecture on Shabbos to the young boys and also during the week whenever someone asked him. He lived to an old age. R' Eeliezer, his only son, married a woman from Mold-Banila, moved there and later on moved to Chernovtsy.

R' Eliezer (son of Ranche) Rosenthal was a tremendous scholar, belonged to Kosov's Chasidim, was a merchant, then later a teacher.

R' Eliezer Shtal. R' Alter Shlomo Yitzchak, his son-in-law, was an old scholar and the Chazan for 'Kol Nidre' and 'Neila'(the first and last prayers on The Day of Atonement) at the Kosov's Synagogue.

Izidor Orenshtein, Principal of "The Baron Hersch School" and a well respected teacher.

R' Anshel Ruven Rubin, one of the veterans and important house owners, well respected man, he participated in many charities. He had a large general merchandise store where his wife, Chayke, also worked. She was a modest good hearted woman who gave a lot to charity. Their children, too continued in their parents way of charity and contributing to the community.

R' Anshel Ruven (Rubin) Family (Eldest Son)

R' Leibel Rubin, their eldest son, was a scholar who dedicated his life to learning. His wife and children provided a livelihood from their store. He was a sick man who suffered greatly and died young.

Shmuel (see below) & Meir Rubin, their sons, studied Torah.

R' Anshel Ruven (Rubin) Family (2nd Son)

R' Tzvi Rubin, the second son, an honest Chasid inherited the house. He prayed in Kosov's synagogue.

R' Aaron Rubin, his only son, was his heir. He died young and his wife, Freimche, a very smart and capable woman took over his business.

R' Anshel Ruven (Rubin) Family (Daughter Karsel)

Etti, his daughter married R' Moshe Yehuda Karsel who was a great scholar with a sharp mind, well versed in all the Jewish Law books. He was a descendant of the righteous R' Yehuda Oierbach, the author of "Mechokek Yehuda" printed in Lwow in 1892. He belonged to the Kosov's Chasidim, prayed in their synagogue, was a Chazan there and involved in internal politics. Towards the end of his life he used to teach young boys at his home, among them myself, Yudel Tolinger and more. It was a large, airy and very well-lit house. He taught Gemara, and Agada and it was a great pleasure listening to his stories. Like all scholars, his wife Etti provided their livelihood. She was a modest woman, who dealt in Lime and Cement with her daughters.

R' Anshel Ruven (Rubin) Family (Daughter Karsel: Eldest Son)

R' Avraham Kersel, their eldest son was a scholar, but was very sick and died at the age of 24 after swimming in the river during the cold winter. He left a young wife with two children: Freida and Yechiel Mechel Kersel who were raised by their aunt Rachel and her husband R' Getzel Weiss (see 15.4 below) while she emigrated to Eretz Yisrael and settled in Zefat where she remarried and passed away there. Yechiel Mechel Kersel Died of Typhus in 1916 in Zablotow, survived by his wife, Feiga, and six children. She brought them up by herself and from her house came the first pioneers from Zablotow to Eretz Yisrael. Esther emigrated in 1922 and settled in Emek-Yizrael. Getzel, Rachel and Avraham followed and Feiga herself followed her children and died here May 5th 1942 (33

Ba'omer, 18 of Eyar). All their descendants are living in Israel and are well rooted in the community and industry.

R' Anshel Ruven (Rubin) Family (Daughter Karsel: 2nd Son)

R' Feibish Karsel, the second son, was a great scholar and a follower of the Kosov's Chasidim. He moved to Kosov with his family where he had a store and enjoyed great success in business, became a distinguished member of the town, but did not stop learning and raised his children up in this tradition. Efrayim Karsel, his son, settled in Chernovtsy and was a permanent writer of the local Jewish Press there. Moshe Karsel, the second son, settled in Kosov and became a famous scholar and a wealthy man. The whole family perished in the holocaust of 1942.

R' Anshel Ruven (Rubin) Family (Daughter Karsel: Daughter)

Their daughter, **Chana**, married R' Avraham Haber, a Chasid of the Kosov dynasty. They inherited her father's Lime and Cement dealership and lived comfortably. R' Avraham died fairly young. All their descendants who remained in the Diaspora perished in the Holocaust.

R' Kopel Haber, their eldest son, dealt in Lumber after his marriage, but was unsuccessful and emigrated to the United States where he was active in the Organization of Former Residents of Zablotow in New-York and other community activities. He was a community tax collector, later served as a Rabbi and a lecturer in one of the synagogues in New-York. He too, like his father, died fairly young.

R' Natan Haber, the second son, was very well versed in general knowledge. He married Tova, the daughter of the great scholar R' David Tzvi Shochet, and they moved to Mikulitchin in the Karpatian mountains where they had a general goods store and dealt in lumber. Later they opened a large and successful restaurant. One son studied Engineering at the Lwow College. he second son became the Secretary and Bookkeeper of the Village Committee despite the fact that the Chairman and all the others on the committee where Anti-Semite Ukrainians. Two sons, Zelig and Fishel Haber, emigrated to Eretz Yisrael where Zelig was later killed during the War of Independence of 1948. They also had one daughter.

R' Anshel Haber, the third son, moved to Vienna during the First World War where he opened a store and was successful. He studied Torah and educated his children accordingly. Ten years ago (1939) the whole family emigrated to Eretz Yisrael where he continued learning Torah while his children supported him until he died in 1946 in Tel-Aviv.

R' Baruch Haber, the fourth son, like his brother lived in Mikulitchin where he was a lumber dealer. He had children who were educated in Torah and general knowledge.

Chayke, their only daughter, married a relative, R' Menachem (Mendel) Haber. During the First World War they emigrated to Vienna, where he opened a store and was successful. After the War they returned to Stanislav where R' Mendel succeeded in a few dealerships and had a large house. They had a few children. Moshe Yehuda is living in Tel-Aviv, Israel.

R' Anshel Ruven (Rubin) Family (Daughter Karsel: 2nd Daughter)

Gitel, their second daughter, married R' Yehoshua Friedel who was a tall man, an expert in languages. They lived at her parents' house and had a small grocery store where she worked. At the beginning the store provided sufficient income but after a few years the expenses grew, and in accordance with the custom that an unsuccessful man becomes a teacher, R' Yehoshua started teaching Gemara, Torah and Jewish script. Despite being a tall and a strong man, he fell ill and died fairly young. They had a son and a daughter. Gitle remarried (despite having a scar on her right cheek from spilt boiling water) to a landowner in a village next to Storozinec in Bukovina District. He like her and her diligence. She ran an inn with many guests, and participated in charities all her life. Leibel, her son (from R' Yehoshua Freidel) married the daughter of R' Chaim Maher and moved to the United Sates.

R' Anshel Ruven (Rubin) Family (Daughter Karsel: 3rd Daughter)

Tzvia, the third daughter, married R' Yehoshua Haber (a relative of his brother-in-law R' Menachem Haber). Their livelihood was made by their steel store in the city market. They had a few children. Tzvia moved to Israel to be with her daughter Chayke (see below), but later returned to Zablotow where she died. Chayke, their only daughter, married N. Reiber from Nepolokovtsy and moved to the United States. They became Zionists, emigrated to Israel, settled in Gan-Yavne where they had an orchard, grew vegetables and had a chicken farm.

R' Anshel Ruven (Rubin) Family (Daughter Karsel: Eldest Son)

Rivka, the youngest daughter, married a successful businessman from Kolomyja and moved there.

R' Anshel Ruven (Rubin) Family (2nd daughter)

Rachel, the second daughter of R' Anshel Rubin, married R' Getzel Weiss, who was well respected and donated to charity. She was very much like him. They were very successful with their wool and silk store. Although barren, they supported their close family and adopted a few young orphans from their family, whom they considered their own. They were all properly educated in school and R' Getsel made sure they all received their dowry and all other requirements. They raised them until they married and continued to support them even after. Some of these orphans are: Shmuel, her nephew (son of her brother Leibel Rubin. See

15.1 above) who was five at the time. Yechiel Mechel , a grand-son of her sister Etti and R' Moshe Yehuda Karsel (see 15.3 above) who was of approximately the same age. Freida, his sister. Feiga, her husband's niece from his brother R' Avraham Weiss. R' Getsel admired R' Yankele and his son R' Mendel from Zablotow. He Prayed in their synagogue all his life and served as the first Gabay. He donated a Torah scroll to the synagogue in honor of his wife and himself.

R' Meir Karsel (a brother of R' Moshe Yehuda. See 15.3 Above), a simple honest man, was a leather dealer. His wife dealt in oil. Avraham Karsel, his son, Moved to Naduvrna where he was a general trader. R' Chaim, the second son, lived with his parents and had a share in the leather business. They lived not far from three synagogues and he used to run into all three every day to participate in a prayer in each one, even in the cold winters. His main synagogue was the Kosov, where he had possession of the Weekly Maftir. R" Yehuda was a scholar who occasionally had articles in the Magid and left Zablotow as a youngster. He may have emigrated to the United States. R' Mechel who died very young was a genius. Meir, Yitzchak and Yehoshua were all killed by the Germans.

R' Isaac Boimel. A respected man, learned, a Chasid of R' Mendele from Demycze and used to pray at the Viznica's synagogue. Had a large house at the center of town. Used to lend money to the people from town and farmers in the area. His son rented a farm in Voytsekhovitse, was a Chasid like his father. Son-in-law R' Moshe Yupiter, learned, a Chasid of the Rabbi of Demycze, and used to read weekly from the Torah on Shabbos in the Viznica's Synagogue. Was a money changer for Jews and Gentiles. R' David, an educated, and a vigorous learner. Although he did not receive a formal trade education, he established a store for steel products in his grandfather's house and became very successful in a very short time. He had a great advantage whereby buyers found him to be very honest and reliable. Was a Chazan in Viznica synagogue and a very accepted member of the community. Tzvi (Hershke) Yupiter, a land dealer and for a short time also had a brick factory and traded in firewood.

R' Avraham Voltzer, a wealthy man, had a large stone house in front of the market with a large wine and whiskey cellar. Was a partner in Profanation (see 19 below) as a bartender and inn-keeper. Carriages of guest and passers-by were always parked in his large yard, especially during market days. Neta Voltzer. Sons-in-law R' Yakov Tau and Kalman Shapira.

R' Efrayim Menashe Shocher, a tall man with a long white beard across his chest. A scholar, very knowledgeable in bookkeeping and served as trustee of the Profintion for most of his life.

Profanation – is the privilege to be a sole distributor of wine, whiskies and Beer, which was handed by the local landowner ("Paritz") who kept those privileges for generations. The Polish government invoked those privileges in 1878 when the commissioner in Lwow for three years at a time rented them out after a public tender. Only wealthy people won them since it required a special building to sell the drinks, rooms for bookkeeping, warehouses, blending and distillation rooms, managers, clerks, secretaries, bartenders, guards, watchmen to prevent outside merchandise from entering, and many servants.

Trustee in those days meant an honest man, smart and knowledgeable in reading writing and bookkeeping.

Efrayim Shocher had all of these qualifications. He was the manager, the bookkeeper, the secretary, the seller and the buyer. He had all the people required. The lessees and renters had no knowledge about the commercial aspects of the business till they received their share when the end of yearbooks was prepared. Profit was large since they were allowed to set prices as they wished. R' Efrayim remained the Trustee although Lessees where changed from time to time. He was one of the "generals" of the rabbi of Viznica and the secretary of the "R' Meir Ba'al Ha'ness" Charity Funds collected in the vicinity including in Viznica. He, his sons and grandson lived in Demycze, all prayed regularly in synagogues in Demycze. He had sons and daughters, all educated in the Torah way.

R' Nachman Shocher.

R' Moshe Shocher

R' Rephael Shocher

R' Chaim Shocher

R' Efrayim Fond, was a great scholar very knowledgeable in the bible, book and paper goods seller. Since this trade did not provide sufficiently, he was also a teacher and taught eight young boys all the Jewish subjects and Hebrew grammar. His lectures lasted all day and each of his students was proficient in all these subjects. His sons too were properly educated in Torah and general knowledge. R' Yitzchak Fond, a smart and knowledgeable man, and very respectable leather merchant. Immigrated to the United States where he lived comfortably. R' Moshe Fond, a smart and knowledgeable man, moved to Kolomyja where he made his livelihood with his brothers-in-law in the brick industry. R' Yeshaya Fond immigrated to Canada where he died at a very young age.

R' Eelkana Kogler, A pious Jew, a Viznica Chasid with a large general merchandise store, was one of the more important citizens of town who donated generously to charities. Educated his sons in Torah and general knowledge too. Did not live long and died at mid-life.

R' Aryeh Leib Rosenboim, a respectable and knowledgeable man, had a house with a wall and dealt in general merchandise. Impoverished lately and forced to sell his house, he became a broker.

His beautiful daughter married R' Avraham'che Oyerbach.

R' Aryeh Leib Melamed, owned a small house in an alley and traded in wheat. His wife sold flour and eggs from the house. Gave their children a Torah education. Eliezer Melamed, worked with his father in the business. After the death of his parents he moved with his wife Beila, daughter of R' Shlomo Salpeter, and their family to the United States where he made a living in commerce.

Mr. Izidor Reizel, Finished his studies in Lwow University, returned to Zablotow as the property manager for the Government Courts. The Judges treated him with respect. He excelled in his community activities, was well respected and behaved as expected from a religious man. Was once elected by the District Governor to be the Jewish Community Leader.

R' Asher Zilberman, came to Zablotow with a group from Zorov in Russia where he was a bookkeeper and accountant for a Whiskey distillery, with R' Yisrael Friedman. Purchased a large house in Demycze, opened a grocery store, donated to charities and had no children.

R' Tzion, the son of R' Chaim Toy, graduated from the Hebrew academy of Rabbi Dr. Yung in Krakow. Studied Jewish and general subjects at his home, was active in community matters especially Zionist oriented, and was one of the first to work with the younger generation to bring them up with the love of Torah, the Jewish-People and the Land of Yisrael. Was a merchant all his life and for a while was considered to be a rich man. Did not emigrate to Eretz Yisrael and was killed with the others in 1942.

R David Kalir, an educated man, a bookkeeper and employee of the "Rosenbaum Bank". A respectable, honest man involved in public activities for the community and Zionist causes. Educated his children in Torah on one side and general knowledge on the other.

R' Hersh Nusberg, an honest merchant educated his children in Torah and general knowledge and was among the contributors to the community.

R' David Toy, son of Yoseph and Chana, an honest man who had a large house with a tavern. His son-in-law R' Shmuel Sharf from Kolomyja, inherited his house and tavern.

R' Zev Shatenfeld, R' Simcha Shochet's son-in-law, a respected and honest person who had a grocery store attached to his house. He educated his children in Torah and general knowledge. Later sold the house and moved to Kolomyja.

R' Zaide Altman, Son of R' Mandel, was educated in Cheder and continued studying Torah and Gemara. Following his marriage he moved to Gankovtsy where he became a general merchant. Educated his children in the honest and proper way.

R' Zalman Mintzer, lived for many years in Popiyelniki, where he was a farmer and a general merchant, accumulated some property and gave to charities. Moved to Zablotow following the murder of his father by local farmers due to his improper activities (such as; loan sharking) and many court trials, where he continued for a while in merchandising but lost everything and became a beggar and lived off handouts till his death.

R' Zanvill Grunvorg, a Kosov Chasid, and a land dealer. Raised his children in the proper way.

R' Gedalya Shafer, a learned merchant. Inherited R' Alter Leibel's position as a public teacher on Shabbos in the old synagogue. R' Alter Shafer was a merchant. His wife, daughter of Mooki Feivels had no children and died young.

R' David Zinger, son of R' Chaim Zimel Zinger, moved to Germany following his marriage. His children were educated in general knowledge and immigrated to Israel.

R' Hendel Shechter, R' Leibel Rubin's son–in-law, a scholar God-fearing Jew who barely survived from his grocery store. Was a Viznica Chasid and became a successful slaughterer in the town of Shatz in Bukovina. His son-in-law R' Berl was also a slaughterer in Cheresh in Bukovina.

R' Davis Tau, son of R' Shmuel, was a wealthy man, a merchant and a moneylender. Was probably the first who used the Pruth River to deliver wood. Till then they used rafts to bring the wood from the Karpathian Mountains. He purchased the wood destined to Rumania from the merchants, got them from the river onto his large yard where his craftsmen built two roomed wooden houses. He sold these houses at good profits, by payments plan and some Jews even purchased them.

R' Eliezer Adlershtein, a respected citizen who prayed at the Kosov synagogue. Had the sole salt dealership from the government factory in Kosov and Delyatin. Emigrated to Eretz Yisrael in his old age with his wife and lived in Zefat.

R' Chaim Zev Blushtein, A scholar who sat and learned Torah day and night. His wife Kani was a good-hearted person known for her good deeds. At the beginning R' Chaim was a "trustee" (see 19 above) at the Semakovtsy Whiskey distilleries and a bookkeeper and accountant at his brother-in-law's business, R' A.V. Meltzer. Later he moved to Zablotow to his house in Demycze. His capable wife opened a grocery store, which provided them with their income. They educated their children in Torah and general knowledge.

R' Moshe Blushtein, the eldest, a scholar, was a merchant then emigrated to the United States and made his livelihood in commerce.

R' Shlomo Blushtein a scholar who had a store in his father-in-law's house R' A. L. Shfarber. Participated in daily learning despite his business troubles.

R' **Yitzchak Isaac Blushtein** his eldest, was a brilliant scholar and one of the pioneers of Zionism in Zablotow. Later lived in Kolomyja where he lived in poor conditions.

R' **Moshe Bley** was his son-in-law. He was a great scholar in Torah and general studies including science and research. Was a teacher for some boys in town.

Tzvi Bley lives in Israel.

R' Avraham Bloch, R' Chaim's first son-in-law, was a Chasid of the Kosov's Rabbi. He had a large business dealing in forest, lumber, houses and land in the vicinity of Delyatin. Has a general merchandise store, which brought him a hefty income. Was known for his charity and hospitality.

His sons, R' Shabtel, R' Yehoshua and others were successful as lumber dealers and owned a few sawmills.

R' Avraham Yitschak Shocher, the second son-in-law was a great scholar, and well respected in Kolomyja. For a long time he was the chief bookkeeper for the "Acsis" which was the company with the monopoly of collecting duties on Meat and slaughter. A group of wealthy men purchased the monopoly from the authorities for a few years and they found R' Avraham Yitzchak to be their most trusted and capable man to ran their business. After leaving that post he dealt in lumber and together with others he purchased a large forest in Bukovina. It was a very successful venture in which he continued for the rest of his life. His Wife Miriam, concentrated in charities, supported the needy, the infirm etc. His sons were educated in Torah and general education, most of them became Doctors and Lawyers.

Dr. Shmarya Shocher his son

Dr. Chana Shocher his daughter is practicing in Jerusalem.

Engineer M. Berler his grandson is employed by the Worker's Union and resides in Jerusalem.

R' Chaim Walfram, a scholar who owned a General Store where his wife and daughters worked. It was the largest store in town with Jewish and Gentile patrons from town and the surroundings. R' Chaim behaved as a Chasid and belonged to the Chortkov's Chasidim. Gave generously to charities. Rabbi Mendele Walfram was one of his sons.

R' Chaim Zimel Singer, a well respected man, a scholar, form the important members of the Kosov community, used to read the Torah, was a wonderful Chazan during the High Holidays, and was Mayor and chairman of the community for a while. His large home housed a tavern, which was usually full with men drinking whisky, wine and beer. In his cellar he had the most sought after Kosher for Passover wines.

R' Yehuda Singer a scholar, 'afflicted" with a little general knowledge Prayed in Kosov synagogue and excelled as a Chazan there during the High Holidays with his soft and pleasant voice. This was despite living in Tulukov where he rented a tavern and owned some land. Was amongst the largest merchants and exporters. R' Yoseph Halpren, his son-in-law was R' Moshe Sheiner Halpern's son, first lived in Vienna then in Tel-Aviv. Died in mid-life.

R' Chail Ber Ebenshtein, a scholar in Torah, an excellent Tanach teacher.

R' Chaim Roysner, R' Yeshayahu Shechter's son-in-law, was an important merchant.

R' Chaim Shetner from Kuti, knowledgeable in general science, was a merchant in Zablotow together with his father-in-law R' Moshe Sheiner (see 41.1.1 above). Immigrated with his wife Esther to Berlin where he was successful in commerce. Was a Chasid, opened a synagogue in his own house, and was known for his hospitality and charity all his life. Educated his children in Torah and general knowledge. Was among those killed by the Nazis.

R' Chaim Hirsh Perchase Greif, a merchant, a Viznica Chasid. Had a large house, but no children.

R' Chaim Locker, owned a large house, dealt in leather and wool clothing from the local farmers. Was well respected and belonged to the Kosov's Chasidim. Educated his sons in Torah and general knowledge.

R' Chaim Deitch (Family name or a nickname), owned a large house in the center of town (which was sold to R' M. Sheiner after his death) and was a wheat dealer. Educated his sons in Torah and general knowledge. R' Alter his son, inherited the house and the business.

R' Yehuda Bloch, son of R' Menachem Bloch, a Kosov Chasid who had an unsuccessful business of soap and candles. Remarried to a woman from Delyatin, moved there but was still unsuccessful the rest of his life.

R" Yehuda Treter, worked for a long time in R' Chaim Walfram's (see 40 above) store. After his marriage with Tzipora he opened his own successful store in his father-in-law's house. Was accepted in the community and educated his sons in Torah and general knowledge. His wife Tzipora was a capable woman who helped in the store.

R' Yoseph Shafer, a homeowner and merchant, was caught in a felony. After his repentance he became honest and charitable. Educated his sons to be honest merchants.

R' Yakov Gleikshtern (Yankel Bomes) owned a house in Demycze next to the Jail, was a Kosov Chasid, prayed there and was a Chazan and a known singer in the synagogue. Was a successful wheat dealer and educated his sons in Torah and general knowledge. R' David Gleikshtern graduated from Teachers College and was a teacher in Baron Hirsh School in Kolomyja. Following his marriage to Eta, daughter of R' Meshulam Simcha Linder, he inherited a large house in Kolomyja, left his teaching position to open a large successful store of wool and silk fabrics. Educated his son and daughter who were great students, in Torah and general education. The Nazis killed the whole family in 1942.

R' Yitzchak Fond, son of Manche, was a relative and a student of R' Efrayim Fond and absorbed his teachings. Married a farmer's daughter, moved to the farm and became a successful farmer and land dealer.

R' Yisrael, son of Shlomo, an honest scholar and a Chasid who made his livelihood as the only one in town sawing leather for shoemakers. Was known for his honesty.

R' Yitzchak, son of R' Hirsh Leib Zeinreich, was a scholar, and a son-in-law of R' Tzvi the son of Yakov Toy. Moved to Vienna during First World War and became a successful merchant. Was an honest man and educated his sons in Torah and general knowledge.

R' David Keish was educated by R' Efrayim Fond. His stepson was a scholar and among the most enthusiastic Chasidim of Kosov, participating in daily lectures. Following his marriage they moved to Kolomyja where he opened a store. Educated his son in Torah. Immigrated to the United States and brought his parents over.

R' Yitzchak Isaac HaCohen Meltzer, an honest simple man from the "generals" of Rabbi Chaim from Kosov. His wife, Tova Shprintze was modest and righteous. R' Yitzchak owned a large property and a mill in Chlebiczim next to Zablotow, and rented land and forests. Both were famous for their generosity, hospitality and charity to the poor. In their house they had rooms and a kitchen exclusively for hospitality. Their children continued to be at home table after their marriages as long as they lived in Chlebiczim.

R' David Meltzer, a scholar and a Chasid rented a farm. His wife Beila, was a daughter of the Rabbi of Kuty. Following his father's death he moved to Torichi and later to Zablotow. In his old age he immigrated to Israel where he became the Chairman of Kosov's Kolel (Jewish school for married men). He held this position for 15 years till his death (rumored to be caused by hunger and his wife too) during the First World War. They were buried in Zefat.

R' Yoseph, a Scholar and a Chasid of Chortkov, moved to Kolomyja following his marriage and opened a leather wholesale store with his father-in-law and became an important member of the community. Lived in Israel 12 years.

Eidel his daughter and her husband R' SH. Sheiber emigrated to Israel together with her father R' Yoseph. All their children excelled in their work and contributed to the land and people of Israel.

Dr. Chaim Sheiber, a former head of a department in Beilinson Hospital in Petach-Tikva, who held important medical positions during the First World War and the War of Independence.

Binyamin Sheiber, a merchant. His wife was a granddaughter of the chief Rabbi of Lwow, R' Moishe.

Berl Sheiber a member of Kibbutz Eilon.

R' Shalom HaCohen Meltzer, a scholar and generous man. Left Zablotow following his marriage and settled in Rohatyn where he became famous for his generosity, were a member of City Council and an important member of the community.

He built the first Jewish school and established a charity fund to help support the needy. He was among the founders (together with R' Feivel Shreyer from Borohotshani and Dr. A. Zaltz from Tarnow) of "Ahavat Zion". This was the first society in Galicia dedicated to the settlement of Eretz Yisrael, which established the village of Machanayim in Israel.

When Theodor Hertzl became an active Zionist, so did R' Shalom. He was a very active Zionist in Galicia, was a delegate to the Second Zionist Congress and at his own expense, traveled around Galicia persuading people to join Zionism. He established "Carmel" Society in Lwow selling Eretz-Israel's Wines. Died young, before the age of forty and was not himself successful to emigrate to Eretz Yisrael.

Dr. Natan Meltzer, one of the top organizers of the "Federation" in Galicia and a dedicated politician of the Worker's Union in Israel.

Rachel, living in Tel-Aviv.

R' Yoseph Meltzer. Following his father's death he moved to Kuty to his father-in-law, R' Zecharya Shtein, and later to Zabie. He was successful in lumber.

His daughter and a few grandchildren are in Israel participating in building the land.

R' Shmaryahu Meltzer was a scholar known for his wealth and modesty. Owned two properties in Chortkov District and was known all around Chortkov and Tarnopol districts for his charity and good deeds. The entire family and its fortune were destroyed during the holocaust.

R' Chaim Meltzer, a scholar managed his wealthy brother's business books and bookkeeping. His son and grandson are living in Israel

Creindel Meltzer married R' Yoseph Shatner who was a Scholar fluent in several languages. During R' Yitzchak Isaac Meltzer's life he rented a farm in Zablotow and owned a whisky distillery. Following R' Yitzchak's death he moved back to his home town Kuty where he opened a wool and silk fabric wholesale store and became famous for his honest business dealings. Their house was always open to the needy and the poor, made famous especially by his modest wife Creindel. He was Chairman of the Kuty community and died in Austria during the First World War. All his sons and grandsons are loyal to their nation, religion and land.

R' Yakov.

A grandson, **Berl Locker,** was the founder of "Poalei Zion" in Galicia and the publisher of its newspaper. Now he is the chairman of the Jewish Agency and one of the leaders of the Worker's Union. Known also as an author and publisher.

A few grandsons are living in Israel:

Dr. Yitzchak Shatner. A specialist and important researcher in Geography and Cartography.

Dr. CH. Shatner. A Medical Doctor specialist.

Miriam Meltzer married R' Shimshon Choen, a scholar from Korolevka. Following R' Yitzchak Isaac's death he moved back to Korolevka to become a wheat dealer. He and his wife were known for their charity and educated their children in Torah and general knowledge. His daughter and grandsons are living in Israel building the land. Dr. A. Lebel, a grandson lives in Gan-Yavne with his daughter.

Rivka Meltzer married R' Menachem Yitzchak Rosenshtroich from Bukovina. They excelled in Charity and benevolence, their home in Lots was always open to the needy.

Tova and her sons are living in Israel.

Engineer A. Kler, a grandson, owns the "Argaman" factory.

R' Yehoshua Preminger, owned a large house, was rich and well respected in town and was a Viznica Chasid. Used to lend money to local farmers.

R' Zalman Preminger owned a successful farming store.

R' Yosel Preminger was rich, owned a Fabric Store and was known for his wisdom

R' Yoseph Koren, his son-in-law, was one of the first Learned Zionist in town between the two World Wars. He owned a hotel and a tavern but was always busy with community work and Jewish culture. He had a magnificent Jewish library. He and his whole family were killed in the Holocaust.

R' Yehoshua Miller, a modest man, knew how to learn Torah, prayed in Kosov's synagogue, read the Torah sometimes and was a Chazan. Inherited his father-in-law's house including a boarding house, a place for carriages and a tavern where his wife and daughters always worked.

R' Yoseph Ruven Shechter, a scholar, had a house and used to lend money to local farmers. Faltered in his business and was caught in a felony.

Reuven Shechter, a scholar. Left Zablotow settled in Yablonov where he was a Gemara teacher.

R' Zeinvil Shechter was a rabbi in a village in the Karpathian Mountains.

R' Yeshaya Shechter had a grocery store then later was a teacher.

R' Shimon Shechter. Already as a young boy was known for his wisdom and good memory, became a teacher but did not practice and hardly made a living. Between the two World Wars was a Gemara teacher. Was honest and modest, never had money and was a perfect example of good behavior.

R' Yoseph Gold had a house in Demycze and owned a sesame seed oil factory. Used to Pray at the Kosov synagogue where he was Chazan on Shabbos.

R' **Yoseph Shpinner,** owned a house and a large lumber warehouse including roof shingles, and boards. Was one of the more successful in that business. He and his wife donated to charities all their lives and supported the needy. Elyahu Shpinner joined his father in the business and later inherited it. Anshel and Lena Shpinner were killed in the Holocaust in 1942 and 1943.

R' Yoseph Balan owner of the Town's Bathhouse was a Kosov Chasid. His brother, Zev Balan was top in this field. They both were honest city attendants and well respected.

R' Yoseph Keish HaLevi, a scholar was an attendant at the Kosov synagogue for a long time. When this did not provide sufficient earnings he weaved fringed garments (Tzitzit) and had many customers from the synagogue.

R' Yoseph Tilinger, a successful grain merchant.

R' Shmuel Tilinger, his eldest, was a great scholar, God fearing Chasid, extremely knowledgeable in the Torah and Rabbinical dynasties. Between the Wars was a Gabay at R' Chaim Hager's synagogue.

R' Mordechai Tilinger was a merchant who moved to Kolomyja following his marriage.

R' Yitzchak (Etche) Tilinger was educated on Torah and general knowledge. Became a lumber dealer and owned land. Was an excellent Chazan on the High Holidays at R' Chaim Hager's synagogue where he sang from his own melodies. Was very smart and well versed in German literature.

R' Yitzchak Tillinger, R' Yoseph's brother, was a very respected man a general merchant and a Gabay in the main synagogue for many years.

Figure 4
R' Yissachar Toy

Yehuda Tillinger, his only son, was educated in various Cheders, excelled in his studies , was very smart, had a sharp mind and good memory, but was light headed. Following his marriage he concentrated on general studied and languages. Later he left Zablotow, settled in

Vienna where he attended Rabbinical School and befriended R' Tzvi Peretz Chayot, Michael Berkowitz, Y. L. Landau, Dov Wachshtein and others. He successfully continued his studies in more colleges, however, to the dismay of his family, converted to become a priest who preached blasphemy. He authored a booklet full of venomous insults and slander at the Jewish Nation, sighting 'clear proof' to Rholing's statements about Jewish hands being soiled with Christian blood for Passover and other vicious criticism of the Jews. A few years later, this black sheep was discovered by R' Yissachar Toy from Zablotow and by the author Gershon Badder, working as a Rabbi and a preacher at a religious synagogue in New York. It was not clear whether he had repented or used the position as a cover, but G. Badder publicly unveiled his mask by publishing his true identity in the local Jewish and Yiddish paper. Tilinger left his post and disappeared forever. He brought great shame to his family especially his mother who mourned this traitor son (His father died suddenly, maybe out of sorrow).

R' Feivel Angler was R' Yoseph Tilinger's son-in-law. He exported grain all the way to Germany. Was a wealthy man who educated his sons in Torah and general education.

R' Yeshaya Shechter, a grocer, was Zelig Adlershtein's partner in government's salt marketing. Despite the long walk to the old synagogue, he used to walk there daily in order to pray in a Minyan (Ten people). In his old age he emigrated to Eretz Yisrael and died in Zefat. 65.1 His sons were Yoseph, Meir, Tzvi and Zev.

R' Yehuda Tzvi Rosenboim, owned a house and had a business in agriculture. His wife was a daughter of R' Avraham Yitzchak Garfunkel (see below).

R' Mordechai Rosenboim worked with his father. His son emigrated to Eretz Yisrael from Germany.

R' Gershon Rosenboim was a scholar and an honest merchant.

Menachem lives in Israel with his wife Devora, daughter of R' Mordechai Keish. During the Second World War was among the brave soldiers who fought Hitler Y"S. He was captured by the German and was held in captivity for a few years. Now living in Kfar Ziv, Tel-Mond.

R' Avraham Yitzchak Garfunkel was an honest Chasid who together with his wife Chaiche, owned a large store selling steel products.

R' Yeshaya Bartler, a Scholar a student of R' Yecheskel Itzik from Kolomyja. Together with some partners he owned "Profanation" (see above). Was a distinguished man in town, prayed in Kosov synagogue. R' Moshe Bartler a scholar, lumber merchant. Emigrated to Eretz Yisrael in 1948 with his wife and one son, who survived the war. Chana, R'

Moshe's daughter emigrated to Eretz Yisrael and became a member of Kibbutz Ashdot-Yakov.

R' Yeshaya Adlershtein, a well respected scholar who rented an agricultural farm and was a partner with R' Eliezer Bartler (a brother of Yeshaya Bartler, see 68 above) in Forestry. They had business connections with Agafsowitch from Tulukow. They had a large forest in Bukovina. His son, R' Eliyahu Adlershtein, rented the large mill in Zablotow. R' Natan Adlershtein was a car dealer in Tel-Aviv.

R' Meir Elazar Sheinhorn, owned a large house in the center of town, educated his sons in Torah and a little general knowledge in accordance with the times.

His son, **R' Moshe Sheinhorn**, who had a sharp mind excelled in his studies including 'foreign' studies. Was a practicing Lawyer who provided handsomely for his large family. Was probably the first in town to point the citizens towards political education and general knowledge. He often called for public meetings, most of them in the Central Synagogue; talked publicly about political subjects and attracted listeners. His understanding relations with the youth caused them to venture into new avenues and studies. He practiced what he preached and especially for community institutions. Established the first ever-Jewish school in Zablotow (no Jewish educational institute existed prior to this one). He persuaded the Baron Hirsh School in Paris and Lwow to open a branch in Zablotow for boys and girls. This action caused a clash with the authorities in Sniatin, when the District Minister, Batcherkas Koifman, followed by the majority of the shortsighted citizens objected and tried to prevent the opening of the school. R' Moshe prevailed, and a large and splendid school did open its gates to hundreds of children in a number of grades, who received an education including Torah, Hebrew and local languages. He saved so many children from being ignorant and illiterate. Most of his life he served as the lone chairman of the community, despite his opponents, and was for a while the official registrar of births and deaths in the community, thus providing himself with some income.

Was an admirer of and respected by Rabbis Yankel and Dudke, he prayed in their synagogue, and acted as their adviser. Educated his sons and daughter in Torah and general education, they all excelled in their studies, their public activities, and as successful merchants in their respective towns.

R' Kalman Sheinhorn, R' Moshe's eldest son, knew perfect Hebrew and German despite the fact that no school or Jewish teacher existed in Zablotow between 1840 and 1880 (where Jewish children could learn Hebrew or languages). Was among the best students of Torah and Gemara.

He married the daughter of a rich man from Viznica, moved there and became a successful lumber dealer who had business connections with Russian merchants, and sent lumber rafts from the Karpathian Mountains along the Chermosh River to Russia. He owned vast forests and lumber mills around Miyawa. His products became famous all around Galicia, Bukovina and Russia.

Excelled in honest business dealings. His house was open to the poor and to the needy. His sons were educated in Torah and general knowledge. In his old age he moved to Chernovtsy, capital of Bukovina District where he became famous for his natural talent, as an honest broker and arbitrator in the most difficult conflicts.

R' Shimshom Sheinhorn, Moshe's second son, was fluent in Gemara and local languages. Immigrated to the United States following his marriage.

R' Tzvi Peretz Sheinhorn was among the more educated people in town. Married the daughter of a rich man from Bukovina, opened a successful commercial store in Beramta. Educated his sons in Torah and general knowledge. Did not live long, died in mid life in his village.

R' Yehuda Rubin son of R' Aaron Rubin, was R' Moshe's son-in-law. He was educated in Cheders and also received general education. He was a partner in a linen factory in Stanislavov and made a good living.

R' Zendel was a scholar who received most of his education from his father. Even at a young age he excelled in his studies and distinguished himself from the other boys. For many years he worked in his father's office.

Following his marriage to his father's main political opponent's daughter (R' Tzvi Rata), they immigrated to the United States where, together with his younger brother R' Yakov, he opened the "Sheinhorn Brothers Bank". The brothers were known for their honesty in business and became very successful. Like his father, he was active in community work. Together with R' Yissachar Toy they established the important organization Former Residence of Zablotow in the United States in order to assist their fellow brethren in the United States and in Eretz Yisrael. He was the permanent secretary of the organization.

R' Yakov died young. Emigrated to the United States with his brother Moshe (See above)

Chana (Chanchel) was a good-looking, cleaver girl. Was brought up by her father in the knowledge of Torah and the local languages. Married an educated man but moved back to her father's house following his death. Helped her father in his business and her mother skillfully run the household.

Pessi, the second daughter, educated like her sister, married a scholar R' Neta, from Davideni in Bukovina. He was the respected village secretary despite the fact that the chairman and the rest of the councilors were all anti-Semitic Rumanians. Excelled in all his public and community activities.

R' Meir Rata, a respected man, had a large house in the center of town, was fluent in local languages which made him famous. Had a tobacco business selling Government approved chewing and smoking tobacco. Was also the sole dealer of Lottery tickets in Zablotow and the surrounding towns. Very few Jews had the honor-obtaining license to sell lottery tickets, only those well known and perfectly honest managed to get it. Was well respected among Jews and Gentile alike. Was elected as head of the citizens, a position he held most of his life and was accepted by most citizens for his achievements. Belonged to Kosov Chasidim, followed R' Yankele and used to participate in their gatherings.

His son, **R' Tzvi Rata,** a scholar, had a house next to his father and was in the tobacco business with him. Was involved in the community, prayed in Kosov synagogue and was a Chazan there during the High Holidays and well liked by the congregates. Was considered a Kosov Chasid who did not shy from confronting their opponents. For a long time he was a very active member of the community. His sons were honest and followed his lead in community work, and education.

R' Isaac Rata, a well-respected scholar, moved to Sniatin and obtained a license to deal in tobacco and sell lottery tickets in Sniatin and the vicinity. Had excellent Characteristics and served as a member of the community board for a while.

His son-in-law **R' Isaac Eizenkraft** was a scholar who belonged to the Kosov synagogue, operated a farming business and used to rent boats to cross the Pruth river.

R' Alter Eizenkraft was a scholar and operated a farming business.

R' Yoseph Eizenkraft, owned a popular restaurant. Killed himself during the first "Action" of 1942.

Tzvi, his son, saved his wife and child from the holocaust and managed to get to Israel.

His second son-in-law **R' Litman Reiter,** had a house next to R' Meir's, was a scholar, a Bible teacher, then later a tradesman. One of the important people in the Kosov synagogue. The whole family Immigrated to the United States where he was successful.

R' Gedalya Rata a musician, married the daughter of a well-respected Kosov citizen and moved there. Was a Chasid of Kosov.

R' Menachem Bergman (Ridniker), an old but strongly built, wide shouldered man who owned a tavern and a hostel which had many guests coming and going daily. Carriages moved constantly in and out of the gates. The yard in front of the house served as an entrance to the market for men, women, merchants, dealers, buyer and farmers. The fish market was held in his house on Thursdays and Fridays.

His eldest son **R' Eliyahu Bergman** was an important member of the Kosov Chasidim. Had a few sons and daughters.

R' Lebche Bergman owned a large store in his house in Demycze. Was a Kosov Chasid.

R' Yerachmiel Bergman, a pious Viznica Chasid.

R' Mordechai Bergman was a studious man and a Rabbi somewhere in Bukovina. In his old age he emigrated to Eretz Yisrael and probably died in Jerusalem. A few of his grandchildren live in Israel.

R' Mordechai Leib Bergman was one of the best students in Gemara. Married the daughter of a rich Putak citizen and was very successful in his commercial business and leasing forests. After a while he purchased a large piece of property and forest in Bukovina. Lived a good life and learned Torah.

His son-in-law was **R' Israel Shtein** the son of the famous R' Zecharya Shtein from Kuty. Was friendly with The Rabbi from Chortkov and an important member of his entourage. Donated freely to his family and to others who approached him.

R' Moshele Shtein who inherited his wealth as well as his personality, lived in Stanislavov. Was killed together with his son Itchele during the last war.

R' Yoel Eizenkraft was R' Menachem's son-in-law who inherited his house and business. Was an honest and modest man, a Kosov Chasid.

Moshe Eizenkraft a scholar who married into a rich family in Bukovina and became a famous forestry and lumber dealer. Later moved to Chernovtsy.

R' Moshe Yakov Fishel an old, quiet man who walked daily to the synagogue despite the long distance from his house. Dedicated a large airy room in his house for daily learning with eight other friends from 8:00AM till 9:00 PM. R' Zanvill Fishel owned properties and was a merchant. An honest man who belonged to the Kosov Chasidim.

R' Mendel Altman had a house not far from the tobacco factory which provided his livelihood. Was a Kosov Chasid. R' Meir Rubin, his son-in-law was an honest man who owned a famous bakery.

R' Menachem Maher, an important member of the community. He sat and learned while his wife Reizel, sold wheat and eggs from their house. He was head of the rabbinate in Petashnizin where he answered Halachic questions and arbitrated in fiscal conflicts. Was well respected especially among those praying in the old synagogue where he was a Chazan during the High Holidays. Educated his sons in Torah and general knowledge.

His eldest son **R' Shlomo Maher**, an author, was a Rabbi in Vrelea, Romania.

R' Yoseph Maher owned an oil field and lived in Nadbora.

Yechiel Mechel Meir Maher published a book in Hebrew and was a famous Banker in Kuty. Educated his son and daughter in general knowledge. Died young in Kuty.

R' Chaim a scholar who exported eggs.

R' Zev Maher, author of "Stories and Paintings", a bookkeeper who owned a house in Kuti.

R' Meir was a student of R Efrayim Fond from whom he absorbed the knowledge of Torah and Gemara in addition to his father teachings of Halacha. Had a perfect knowledge of Hebrew. Following his marriage he tried a few commercial businesses but was unsuccessful and became a Hebrew teacher (taught a few boys for free). Was probably the first in town to educate a whole generation of Zionists, was fluent in Hebrew. A few years later immigrated to the United States where he was active in the community, teaming up with other former residents of Zablotow.

R' Mordechai Shfarber, an honest and modest man sat and learned all his life. Had a house on the road to Kolomyja and a store in his brother's house' R' A. L. Shfarber, attended by his wife Rosa and his sons. Was a sick man and died young survived by his wife and four children.

Tzvi Shfarber was educated in Cheder by his mother. Knew Torah, Hebrew and Yiddish and assisted her in the store. Following his marriage he moved into his father-in-law's business in Kuty, where he later inherited the house and the General store.

R' Chaim Shfarber was educated by his mother in Cheders, later inherited her house and store. Educated his sons in Torah.

Dina, one of his daughters, married Moshe Toy, miraculously survived the holocaust of 1942-43and lived in Poland from 1946-47. The Nazis killed all the rest of the family.

R' Moshe Shnaryahu Shfarber had a house and business but lost them and lived off charitable donations. Later, together with God's help, became a successful matchmaker. R' Natan Shfarber was unsuccessful as a Yiddish and German teacher.R" Asher Pasternak, his son-in-law was an honest man, first as a merchant and later as a teacher. Inherited land and a house in Bukovina where he became successful.

R' Menachem Bloch, a pious scholar. At his young age he manufactured candles and soap. Later became a private teacher and taught a few boys. R' Avraham Bloch was an exporter. In his house he had a factory that manufactured pig hair and feather brushes. Educated his sons in Torah and general knowledge. R' Zeide Bloch inherited the business. R' Berish Bloch was a merchant. He lives in Haifa, Israel R' Alexander Shtempler, R' Avraham's son-in-law, was a Torah scholar and a Chazan. He was a banker in Mielchi.

R' Mordechai Tzvi Fogel, a tenacious student of Torah. A young teacher whose talents enabled him to purchase a house and properties. He became a successful land dealer and in sold wood for heating. Later he became a moneylender. His son Zenvill Fogel and the others were very smart. Shlomo and Avraham Fogel were very active in Zablotow's Zionist Movement. Lazil Shtein, his son-in-law, was a scholar who owned a house and a store.

Fisher brothers, R' Mordechai and R' Asher Anshel were important egg exporters to Germany. Both owned houses and R' Mordechai had a wholesale wheat and egg store in his.

R' Menachem Tseichner was a poor and unfortunate man whose wife and father-in-law dominated his life. He had a fish store.

R' Meir Charab, the son of R' Avraham the plasterer had a very sharp mind for Gemara.

R' Meshulam Epshtein, a descendant of a dynasty of Rabbis, behaved like one both at home and in the Kosov synagogue where he was an important member

R' Moshe Epshtein had a store in his father's house. Educated his sons in Torah and general knowledge.

R' Menache Epshtein a scholar who had a soft and pleasant voice and prayed in the Kosov synagogue and educated his children in Torah

One of his sons-in-law was **R' Shmaya Leviner**, a successful forestry and lumber dealer lived in Viznica and later moved to Chernovtsy.

R' Zeide Epshtein was son-in-law of R' N. Dreamer of Nadbora.

R' Aryeh Leibish Eisner, R' Meshulam's first son-in-law, a distinguished scholar very knowledgeable in Halacha who had a very sharp and good memory. Was loved by all especially the Kosov Chasidim who enjoyed listening to his fabulous stories, fables and jokes. Most of the time he lent money to local farmers, and lately also sold wood for heating. Was constantly involved in lawsuits, conflicts and arguments with his clients. Despite knowing just Hebrew he became familiar with the court system and the local Law, especially in damages and monetary matters. Even Judges treated him with respect. He once lost his case, approached the judge and politely explained to him the letter of the law. The judge agreed and overturned his verdict. His interpretation was published and became the Law of the land. His sons were educated in Torah. In his mid life he faltered and cast a black shadow over himself and his soul. A foreign fire burnt in him. He died young as predicted by our sages: "Why do scholars die young?. Because they ridicule themselves".

Israel Eisner did not follow in his father's footsteps, not in Torah nor in knowledge. Later he left Zablotow to the United States.

His other sons were unsuccessful and uneducated.

A second son-in-law was **R' Nachum Orenshtein** who was a scholar and follower of Kosov Chasidim but did not live long in Zablotow. He divorced his young wife, moved back to Chernovtsy where he became a respectable and successful forestry dealer.

R' Moshe Guthartz, had a house and was an important merchant. R' Eliyahu Guthartz was an important merchant. R' Neta Guthartz was a scholar who sold wigs to the Gentiles. Educated his sons in Torah, general knowledge and Jewish identity. Supported Zionism and sent his son Yakov to Eretz Yisrael. He supported him and sent him money to buy a house and land, but Yakov did not succeed which frustrated his father whom died at a young age and did not fulfil his dream to immigrate to Eretz Yisrael. R' Yakov Guthartz emigrated to Eretz Yisrael and was one of the first pioneers of Hertzelya. (his son Amos and family still reside in Hertzelya -1998)

R' Michael, named Korales was a teacher in the old Beit-Midrash on Shabbos. He was an egg wholesaler.

R' Moshe Zanvil's Toy, one of the wealthiest men in town who had business relations with large property owners.

R' Yakov Toy, his eldest son, a wealthy scholar who owned a linen, wool and silk fabric store and a large house in the city market.

R' Tzvi Toy, a merchant who was in agriculture, had a Tavern in Rudniki and used to rent out boats to cross the Pruth river. Later purchased R' A. Oyerbach's house and became an important citizen in town and belonged to the Kosov synagogue.

R' Chaim Toy had a house and a lending-bank. Was a regular at the Kosov synagogue where he also read the Torah. Following R' Chaim Zemel's death he became the head of the Community.

R' Meshulam and Ben-Zion Toy where educated at Dr. Yung's Hebrew Academy.

R' Moshe Toy a scholar and an important merchant in town.

R' Avraham (Bony) Toy was one of the founders of the Chalutz (Pioneer) Youth Movement of Zablotow. He emigrated to Eretz Yisrael but his illness forced him to return to Zablotow where he concentrated on educating the youth in Zionism and love of Israel. He suffocated to death in a train car in 1942.

Son-in-law of R' Yakov was **R' Tzvi Shreyer** who was a respectable leather merchant and important citizen of Bohorodshani. Emigrated to Eretz Yisrael in his later years. His sons were Merchants.

R' Zev Toy a scholar of the Kosov Chasidim. Owned a house and a store for various fabrics, but most of his time was spent learning Torah. Was the first to enter and last to leave the Kosov synagogue. Was considered one of the "Ten Bums" of town (A nickname given to the most serious and devoted). `Practice blowing the Shofar during the whole month of Elul (proceeding the High Holidays). His wailing prayer at the onset of the blowing of the Shofar on Rosh-Ha Shona (New Year day) was heart breaking. His Shofar blowing was loud and trembling. But about making a living? He would rather have it done by others. His very capable, smart and diligent wife, Sassy, "brought home the bread". She was the grocer, the house manager and the teacher of her sons. She had two sons from a previous marriage:

Alexander Rosenboim became an important and successful merchant in Zalishtshiki.

Baruch Rosenboim, a steel merchant in Kolomyja.

She died young survived by her second husband, R' Zev Toy, and three young orphans. After her death the house lost its shine and dwindled till the death of R' Zev. His brother Pesach raised one daughter.

R' Pesach Toy, R' Moshe's third son, was raised by his brother R' Yakov following the passing of both his parents. Was a good hearted man and a scholar. Inherited his father's fortune and married a rich man's daughter from Stanislavov. He moved there, opened a store and a successful wholesale flour warehouse. Was a Chortkov Chasid. During the War of 1914 he, with his family and other refugees escaped to Vienna. Here he was free from his business so he turned to the spiritual and found the cause of the disaster and the end of this world. He found in the book of "Daniel" clues and secrets that the cruel Russians and their righteous corroborators – The Kaiser Franz Joseph and his partner William who emerged as heroes from that terrible war, will bring long lasting redemption to this world. The Jews too will benefit and will return to their homeland. Based on these dreams, fantasies and hallucinations he published a German booklet (probably with the assistance of others) filled with clues and prophecies which he sent to the Court, Ministers, Army Generals and all the worldly, great people of that era. He received thanks, great responses and reviews from them and collected these into a book, which cost him a fortune. He sent it to many of his friends to show how well accepted he had become in the world. If he was mistaken, he was not the first and only one; many before him misled the world with their hallucinations. As a whole he was an honest man, donated large sums to charities and was close to Zionism.

Sara, his only daughter was a very smart woman. She married Dr. Alexander Riterman, a Lawyer who was an enthusiastic Zionist, and for a while, the Mayor and head of the Jewish community of Stanislavov. They dedicated themselves to Zionism and through their persuasion a large house surrounded by ten Dunam (one Acre) of land in the middle of town was purchased for a Jewish day school and for teaching and practicing agriculture. A few dozens boys and girls completed their education here and emigrated to Eretz Yisrael. Sara established the "Rachela" company where Jewish girls were taught Hebrew and handicrafts as preparation for immigration to Eretz Yisrael. She participated in each institution. She visited here in Israel ten years ago, returned abroad with the hope of returning here but was among those killed in 1942.

Her only son, **Reuven** is a Lawyer in Israel.

R' Moshe Tau, son of R' Anshel. A scholar who inherited a house and some land leased to a Gentile. He was a clerk too and a private lawyer but with a limited income. His brother, Neta, inherited some land too. He lived in Il'intse and had commercial ties with the locals.

R' **Moshe Yoseph Dreamer** was a pious Jew, a scholar who owned a large house and a store. Educated his sons R' Chaim and Meir Zeassi in Torah and general knowledge.

R' **Moshe Shechter** (nick-named Polki) was an old Jew, Gabay in Viznica synagogue, and owned a house in Demycze. R' Mordechai Keish was his son-in-law.

R' Moshe Rosenboim, a well respected member of the community, owned a large house in the market square where he ran a hostel and a restaurant for a while then a wine and whiskey store (for the Profanation) with a storage room in the cellar. Leased an agricultural farm.

R' Avraham Rosenboim (Avche) was an innkeeper most of his life. R' Yoseph Spinner was his son-in-law.

R' Eliyahu Rosenboim was a scholar and participated in his father's business, and inherited the house and the business following his father's death. Educated his children in Torah and general education.

R' Yisrael Meir Rosenboim, a scholar, a Chasid and a merchant. Later became a successful manufacturer of Salami in his house.

His son **Alexander** was for a long time a successful jeweler in Germany and now lives in Tel-Aviv.

His wife **Minche**, his sons Yoseph and Avraham were killed.

R' Tzvi (Hershel) Rosenboim a scholar, was employed by a financial institution which he and some of his family had established in town. He excelled as manager, bookkeeper and accountant, and later moved to Kolomyja where he became a merchant. Educated his three sons and three daughters in Torah and general knowledge, completed their college studies with honors, became Doctors and emigrated to Eretz Yisrael. Later moved to Lwow, were an active Zionist and a member of the "Mizrachi". Emigrated to Eretz Yisrael and was in a business with his son Moshe, had Chasidic characteristic, a follower of and a permanent worshiper in synagogue of the Rabbi from Sadagura, R' Avraham Yakov Freidman. Died in Tel-Aviv in 1946. His wife lives with her son Dr. Eliyahu.

His eldest son, **Dr. Eliyahu Rosenboim** was R' Aaron Kahn's son-in-law, was an author in Kolomyja, and is now the superintendent in the Department of the Education of the City of Tel-Aviv.

His second son, **Dr. Moshe Rosenboim** is a manager of the famous factory.

The third son is a medical doctor specialist.

R' David (Berche) Rosenboim was a respected scholar, owner of a large house on the road to Kolomyja. His home housed a tavern and the local courthouse and land-registry office (before the authorities built buildings for that and for a jail).

R' Tzvi (Hershel) Rosenboim, a scholar who moved to Kuty following his marriage and became a banker and was an important citizen, and a member of the Community Board etc.

The fourth son was **R' David Rosenboim,** a scholar with agricultural business and a partnership in Profanation. Had a house next to the train station.

Sara married R' Ovadya Greif, a pious Jew, an enthusiastic follower of the Viznica's Rabbi and a follower of R, Mendele from Demycze. Had a large house and an inn and a restaurant for merchants arriving from far. Educated his sons in Torah and Chasidism. R' Zeide Greif was first a shop owner, later a clerk and bartender at the Profanation. R' Yakov Greif, a scholar, moved to Viznica to his father-in-law's house. R' Tzvi (hersh) Katz, a scholar, was his son-in-law. Was a diligent leather merchant in Kolomyja. Later in his life he moved to Vienna and died there. His son lives in Tel-Aviv.

R' Menachem (Mendel Tchanchick), a pious Jew, a Chazan on holidays in various small communities. Educated his children in Torah and the worship of God. His wife, Meryassi, was a modest trader standing at her booth in the market selling toys and household goods.

R' Mordechai (Motel) Beizer, was R' Zalman Gerstenhaber's son-in-law who was mostly busy studying Torah. R' Mordechai was a scholar, and a respected merchant. His daughter and her husband R' Tzvi Toy lived in Tel-Aviv.

R' Meir Hanish, a scholar and very knowledgeable. Was R' Zalman Gerstenhaber's son-in-law from Il'intse. For a while was working in R' Tzvi Toy Yakob's on the river ferry. Later became a merchant in town and active in community work.

R' Mordechai nicknamed Zeide Vitchi's (namely; the son of the widow Vitchi, who had a large house in the market square). He was a scholar and intellectual. He gazed and got hurt; He was hooked by Missionaries and fled to London, England where he was an active member in their missionary work. His family, especially his mother, tried desperately to save him but was unsuccessful. Suddenly he shocked his mother when he re-appeared in town, repented and returned to Judaism. The joy of his family which accompanied his return was short lived when he got sick and died suddenly a few months later. The elders and women said that he died so soon after his return from London because he fled from his instigators but they had his photo with which they cast a spell on him, then poisoned and burnt the photo. This caused his death in Zablotow. His demise became an example for parents warning their children not to follow in his footsteps. However, those who denied these follies explained that all his family died of Tuberculosis and Pneumonia, and the filthy London air worsened his condition and hastened his death.

R' Moshe Alter, from a Russian family who came with Rabbi Yisrael Freidman from Rucsin. He lived for a while in Dzhurov and had a whiskey distillery. Later he moved to Zablotow where he purchased a large house in Demycze. He was well respected and had vast income from his business in Dzhurov. Educated his children in Torah and general knowledge. Yecheskel Alter moved to Bukovina where he was employed as a manager and bookkeeper of a whiskey distillery. Yehuda Leib Alter. His only daughter married R' Shalom Fuchs.

R' Moshe Greif (Hersh) who was a moneylender to the local farmers. Educated his two sons in Cheder and taught them reading and writing.

R' Yoseph Greif moved to his father-in-law's house in Kolomyja after his marriage, and became a major merchant of grain and flour. R' Efrayim moved to his father-in-law's house in Kosov after his marriage, and became a major merchant of grain and fruit.

R' Moshe Sheiner, owned a house in the center of town (formally R' Chaim Deitch's house), had commercial ties outside the country, dealing in tools, shovels, shears, steel, leather, wool and silk fabrics. Prayed in the Kosov synagogue. Educated his children in Cheders and general knowledge. His son Yoseph Halpern moved to Germany and became wealthy. A few years ago immigrated to Israel, purchased a large house and died in Tel-Aviv in 1946.

R' Moshe Toy, son of Yoseph owned a large house in the center of town, was a merchant and bartender. Prayed in the old synagogue. Educated his sons in Cheders and prepared them for real life. His brother-in-law, was R' Aaron Yosis, a scholar who owned a large house next to his. His son, Chaim Tzvi was for a while an excellent economist for a large property owner in the vicinity.

R' Moshe son of the elder R' Shmuel Yakov, both pious serious Jews, strict in their keeping of the Jewish Laws. Owned a large house in town next to the Polish School. Both were supervisors on agricultural farms. One summer day in 1881 clouds covered the sky, lightning and thunders broke out with heavy rains. Suddenly there was a tremendous noise as if the city had exploded. Then it was discovered that a lightning had struck R' Moshe's house, killing him there. Nobody else from his family, nor his elderly father was injured. His funeral was attended by most of the citizens.

R' Moshe Leib Mimlis moved to Zablotow from Brady on the border with Russia, with two government licenses: One for running a tobacco (Chewing and smoking) store, the only such license in the town and the surrounding villages (approximately thirty in district). The second was for selling lottery tickets for lotteries from Vienna, Berlin and Lwow. Although he was an elderly man he put in a full day's work every day, and was quick in his trade. Behaved as a Kosher Jew and spent each free minute learning Torah (usually the book "Akedat Yitzchak"). Following the tragic death of his son (See below) his fortune did not shine either. A few years later he was accused of embezzlement related to his licenses, was found guilty and sentenced for one year. Whether he was jailed or ran away he disappeared forever and was never seen again in Zablotow. We can pity this men, "Righteous man are scrutinized with a fine comb". The Anti-Semite judges considered a shadow as a mountain. Those who say that he erred are mistaken.

R' Shlomo Iche Mimlis came with his father and had two licenses of his own: One for operating a tavern and a pub in the train station (he was the first Jew to have this). The second was to be the sole purchasing and selling agent for the tobacco factory in town. It was the only factory in Bukovina and Eastern Galicia, it occupied a very large area and provided jobs for hundreds of workers. He wheeled the daily production out of the factory on his carriages even on Shabbos and Holidays. He was an educated assimilated Jew who did not care for Jewish Laws. He educated his children in general knowledge in colleges and public schools, a few of them strayed away to foreign cultures, and it is rumored that two left the Jewish faith. His financial condition was good, but that was not enough. His large house was next to the train station. One night, when he returned home with the daily earning (a small one that day) in his pockets, a young Polish man ambushed him, hit him on the head with a steel bar and killed him. The killer was caught, put on trial and sentenced to 20 years in jail. Most of the citizens accompanied him on his last journey.

R' Noach Altman had a large house with a store near the tobacco factory, where he provided the needs of the factory workers. He was a scholar and a Kosher Jew, who walked daily to the synagogue despite the long distance. R' Moshe Altman was educated in Torah, inherited his father's house and business.

R' Noach Gerstenhaber, son of R' Zalman Gerstenhaber, an honest merchant.

R' Nechemya Shfarber, an old scholar who continued his studies daily following his work.

R' Baruch Shfarber, the eldest son was a great scholar. Following his unsuccessful bid as a merchant he became a slaughterer, moved to the large village of Zabieh in the Karpathian Mountains where he served as a slaughterer, Rabbi and a Chazan. Like his father he was a follower of the Kosov Rabbi.

R' Feivel Shfarber, a scholar, a Kosov's Chasid, a Chazan with a pleasant voice. Following his unsuccessful bid as a merchant he became a slaughterer, too and was well respected in town.

R' David Mechel Shfarber was a scholar, bookkeeper and an accountant for various banks. Moved to Vienna during the war.

His son was considered an assistant of Dr. Sigmund Freud and author of a few articles in Psychoanalysis.

R' Baruch's second son was **R' David Shfarber** was very well versed in Jewish Law, and book researcher. Was elected as Rabbi in Preshov in Hungary. Visited Eretz Yisrael together with R' Chaim the Rabbi of Kosov in 1938, returned home longing to immigrate to Eretz Yisrael but was killed by the Nazis.

R' Shabtel Shfarber, was a scholar who possessed a great knowledge in the new Hebrew literature. For a while was a partner in a store with his brother-in-law R' Aaron Rubin. Later immigrated to the United States with his wife and five daughters where he made his livelihood as a Hebrew teacher.

R' Shaul Shfarber, a scholar, well respected with a large house in Demycze with a store and a tavern. Was a follower of the Kosov Rabbi. His granddaughter lives in Tel-Aviv, Israel.

R' Neta Zeinrich one of the elders of the town and very well respected, an unofficial teacher of the Community Committee, who sat and learned day and night. His modest wife sold flour and eggs from their house and had a comfortable income. R' Tzvi Aryeh (Hirsh Leib) Zeinrich, a scholar, a Viznica Chasid and a follower of R' Mendele from Demycze. Had a leather store where he made a comfortable income. Educated his sons in Torah and general knowledge. They made their way in various vocations. Berish Zeinrich and his family live in Tel-Aviv, Israel R' Netanel Freidman was R' Neta Zeinrich's son-in-law. He was a scholar, a Viznica Chasid. Had a large house next to the Great Synagogue where his wife sold flour and eggs. R' Tzvi (Hershel) Menchel, another son-in-law, a Chasidic scholar, merchant of forestry, leased an agricultural farm and kept moving around to live next to his business. Was unsuccessful and lost his money. R' Moshe was an important merchant but later lost everything and just wandered around.

R' Natan Heikel had a small house in the market square, sold pots and wooden pans in partnership with his brother R' Avraham. They lived like Yissachar and Zevulun whereby R' Avraham sat and learned Torah and R' Neta shared his profits with his brother. Educated their children in Torah. R' Avraham was sick and died in midlife.

R' Natan Keren, a scholar, R' Yakov Toy's son-in-law who had a large lumber warehouse and a large house. Excelled in his work in the community and Zionism. Motel Keren was educated in Torah and was a student in the Hebrew Academy in Stanislavov. The whole family was killed in 1942.

R' Natan Chavtan (Bander), was the only one who manufactured barrels required for eggs export. Was a simple and honest man.

R' Natan son of R' Shlomo Zalman Keish, born in Obertyn. Following his marriage to Freida, the daughter of R' Gershon Shfarber he moved to Zablotow, inherited his father-in-law's house and opened a leather goods store.

The Keish Family was a descendant of the tribe of Cohanim. It is rumored that they had a family tree dating back hundreds years ago, but it was burnt.

R' Natan sold mainly to the local Gentile farmers, his Jewish shoemakers customers adored him, trusted him and respected him. During the slow summers he spent more time learning Torah at home. He was hospitable especially during Shabbos and Holidays. He built the first synagogue for the Hager Dynasty in Kosov and served four generations of the Hager dynasty, financing it on his own. The glorious airy and roomy building stood on the way to Kolomyja and had room for 100 men and 100 women in the gallery. Most of the congregation respected him and on Shabbos came over to his house to have a drink of wine, whiskey, beer, eat cakes and "kugel" and sing Shabbos melodies.

His wife, Frieda had her own linen and salt store to finance her charitable donations. She died in 1886 at the age of approx. 70.

R' Natan was born approximately in 1815 and died in 1888 in Zablotow.

R' Aaron Keish, the eldest, was brought up in Torah and was God fearing Jew. He spent most of his time learning and others provided for his livelihood. Following his marriage to Esther Devora, the entire family was supported for a few years by his father-in-law, R' Yitzchak Isaac Meltzer. After R' Yitzchak's death she opened a grocery store in R' Natan's house providing them with a limited livelihood.

Their first son, **R' Naftali** was an honest man, a scholar who moved to a village in Bukovina with his wife Bracha where he made a living in various businesses. He returned to Zablotow to inherit his father's house and business. Educated his sons in Torah and general knowledge.

David Keish immigrated as a young boy to the United States where he became a successful businessman.

R' Tzvi (Hershel) Keish , a scholar, worked with his father and lived with his wife Tova at his father's home. He died very young after a short illness and his young wife followed too.

R' Natan Keish with his wife Esther inherited his father's large house at the market square, the family property, the agriculture business with Gentile land-renters and was very successful. The entire family was killed in 1942. His son Naftali and his daughter were educated in Torah.

The second son is myself.

The third, **R' Gershon Keish** moved to Peshtnizin with his wife Beila, where he was a successful lumber dealer and farmer. Educated his sons in Torah and general knowledge, they graduated from various schools and colleges and found their way to various vocations. He died in New York in 1937 at the age of approx. 70.

R' David a scholar who moved to the United States following his father's death in 1896. He established himself there and his entire families are living comfortably.

Gitel married R' Yehoshua Shrenzel from Skala on the Russian border. They lived for a few years at R' Aaron's house while he learned Torah with his friends R' Eliezer son of Ranche, R' Shmuel Tilinger and a few other boys (myself among them). He did not get paid for this saying: "Since I live for free so will you". After a few years he moved to Skala, inherited his father's house (a merchant of coral jewelry), educated his sons and daughters in Torah and general knowledge and they became famous in the area.

R' Yisrael Leib Freifelder, his son-in-law was famous for his good qualities, an enthusiastic Zionist, head of the community, deputy head of the citizens and an important politician involved in community work and Zionism. He visited our country and with his wife was on his way to settle in Eretz Yisrael when he was captured by the Nazis and killed.

Naomi (Zisel) and her husband R' Chaim Fidrer live in Tel-Aviv, Israel

Sara Ita married R' Binyamin Dov Gold who was a farmer in the area of the town, Otynya. Sara Ita excelled in charity and supported all who approached her for help. They had five boys.

R' Isaac and R' Chaim died during the first war.

R' Natan, R' Yehoshua and R' Zev immigrated to the United States and made a comfortable living.

Elka married R' Yitzchak Yehoshua Freilich who was a pious follower of the Kosov Rabbi (where he was born), a watch-maker and a jeweler living in the small house he purchased in Zablotow. Elka was a capable woman who assisted him in his business and donated generously to charity. During bad times she went house to house collecting money for the needy and for charities. Educated their sons and only daughter in Torah and the fear of God.

Mordechai Dov Keis, a pious Jew, a watchmaker, moved to Vienna during the first war with his wife and sons where he continued his jewelry business. Emigrated with his family to Eretz Yisrael in 1933 continuing in the same business. His son Mechel and his daughter Devora are living on an agricultural farm.

Tova, daughter of R' Yitzchak, married R' Yisrael Flintshtein was killed by the Nazis in Antwerp, Belgium. Tova and her sons emigrated to Eretz Yisrael where they entered Yeshiva.

R' Aaron David, a scholar studied in The Krakow Yeshiva, married the daughter of Rabbi R' Avraham Yehoshua Heshel from Kopashintsy and is now a diamond dealer.

Naftali studies in a Yeshiva in Bnei-Brak, Israel, is a diamond polisher and lives with his mother in Tel-Aviv.

Leah is working in a dental clinic in Jerusalem, Israel.

R' Natan, a bachelor, died of Typhus.

Tova, Daughter of R' Aaron, married R' Yisrael Shtedler son of R' Eliezer from Arelitz, was brought up on Torah and Chasidism. Following his marriage he and his brother R' Moshe leased large farms near Tulukow and in Sarata. Later they purchased a house and wood storage in Sadagura. The Nazis killed Tova.

Natan and Yehoshua immigrated to South America and became the rich owner of a furniture factory.

Chana and her husband David Shterenberg are living in Tel-Aviv, Israel.

Second son of R' Natan and Frieda Keish was **R' David Keish** who was a scholar and excelled as a musician and a Chazan in the synagogue of Kosov. Following his marriage to Devora, daughter of R' Yehoshua Shtein one of the wealthiest men of Bukovina he opened a successful wholesale and retail wool and silk store. They lost a son and a daughter at a young age. R' David died close to the age of 40 in 1880, while Devora who was a capable woman continued successfully to run his business. She donated most of the furnishing for the synagogue in Kosov as a memorial to her late husband R' David.

Ita married R' Zanvil Kahane son of R' Chaim in Sziget, Hungary. He was a scholar and an offspring of a dynasty of famous Rabbis.

The Kahane family from Hungary was famous for their charity and developing commercial dealings in forestry and lumber.

R' Chaim Kahane's father-in-law was Rabbi Yehuda Moderin, who authored a Halachic book and was a friend of the Rabbi Hillel Lichtenshtein. Both were students of the brilliant and pious Rabbi Moshe Soffer who authored the famous "Chatam Soffer". Rabbi Yehuda Moderin attended his grandson R' Zanvil's wedding in Zablotow. All the citizens honored him. He gave a long lecture during the groom's dinner, which was attended by many who listened to each and every word he said and talked about it for a long time afterwards.

R' Zanvil was his mother-in-law's a partner, as well as with others in various commercial ventures. He was a Kosov Chasid and well accepted in town. They had a daughter and a son named after his grandfather, Yehuda Moderin. However, man's success vanishes like a dream.

His wife died after a short illness, followed by her mother's Devora, death., and business faltered rapidly. One of his partners entangled him in some bad business dealings with a Gentile, resulting in a trial and he was found guilty costing him a fortune to get out of it. He was forced to close the store causing him further losses until he fled with his two children to the United States where he was unable to reestablish himself and died shortly after, followed by his daughter.

Yehuda Kahane his son established a small bank with some partners and made a living.

R' Feivel Rata, a Pious Jew. Chasid from the followers of the Viznica Rabbi and Rabbi Mendele from Demycze. Was familiar with Jewish Law, a knowledgeable mathematician and practiced old-fashioned bookkeeping. Most of his life he was a "trustee" of the town's Profanation, first under the authority of R' Efrayim Menashe Shicher. Following R' Efrayim's death he became the Trustee and the bookkeeper. His son R' Yakov Rata, a scholar, was a bartender most of his life at the Profanation facility. His son emigrated to Eretz Yisrael from Germany. He purchased a house in Sheinkin in Tel-Aviv where he lives with his family. Esther married R' Shimon Hirsh. After their divorce she remarried a hotel owner and restaurateur in Stanislavov.

R' Fishel Rata son of R' Tzvi, one of the important men in town inherited his father's house and business of government licenses to deal in tobacco and lotteries. He was active in community work and in Zionism. R' Yitzchak Isaac, his brother moved to Sniatin following his marriage He too possessed government licenses for Tobacco and lotteries, and excelled in Community work in town.

R' Pertz Sisman, a scholar who owned a large house and warehouse of lumber and roof shingles. Moved with his family to Vienna during the first war where he purchased a forest and a profitable lumber mill. Educated his sons to general knowledge. Died in Vienna. One of his sons was son-in-law of R' Tzvi Toy, son of Yacov Toy.

R' Tzvi son of Anshel Toy, a scholar who owned a house in the market square with a large linen and silk store. Mirche, his wife was a very capable woman who assisted her husband in his business, spent her time working for charities. Educated their children in Torah and general knowledge.

R' Tzvi Grager (a Family name or a nickname), a well respected man dealing in grain. R' Yoseph was his heir and inherited his business.

R' Kalman Shapira, R' Avraham Valtzer's son-in-law, a scholar, grain dealer usually in bulk export. Educated his sons in Torah and general knowledge. After a few years he left Zablotow and returned to Shatz, his birthplace, and to the forestry and lumber business. The family became well known for their honesty, trust and successful merchants. Moved with his family to Chernovtsy in his old age.

R' Ruven Shechetr (Golde Rose's), owned a house with a General Goods Store in Demycze. R' Zalman was educated in Cheder and knew Gemara. Following his marriage he moved to Storozinec where he had a partnership with his brother-in-law, R' Peretz, in kerosene and candles.

R' Shabtay Shteinberg, (Ethel's) owned a house. He and his wife were merchants of flour and grain. His sons, R' Eliezer, R' Avraham, R' Mechel and R' Tzvi were educated in Cheder and became grain dealers.

R' Shimon Drukman, born in Bukovina, had a house in Demycze, was a Chasid and an honest merchant. Educated his children to honesty and was well respected. One of his sons is in Israel.

R' Shlomo Zalman Dolberg, a respectable scholar, who had a large house at the market square. He was a leather dealer. His son, R' Yakov was a scholar. Immigrated to the United States. His second son, R' Mordechai was a watchmaker and jeweler and later immigrated to the United States as well. His sons-in-law were well versed in Torah. One of them, R' Eliezer Ranche's (Rosenthal) was well known in Zablotow.

R' Shmuel Grunworg, a respected scholar, an enthusiastic follower of the Rabbi from Kosov and walked daily form his house out of town to the synagogue. Was an important merchant of grain and properties.

R' Shlomo Shusheim, a scholar familiar with book research. Lectured regularly on Shabbos about Jewish Legends to a large crowd who loved and cherished him He educated a whole generation in the love of Jewish Ethics and morality and to Zionism. Later he moved to Stanislavov where he continued the same activities and joined the Mizrachi Organization. Educated his children in Torah and general knowledge. One of his sons is A.L. Shusheim, a well-known author and publisher who, for a while, published a Yiddish paper in Stanislavov and became famous for laying the foundations for the "Poale Zion" movement. Now he is one of the editors of "the working Eretz Yisrael" paper in Argentina.

R' Shmuel Landau, a scholar. His wife, Krinche, was the daughter of the rich Chasid R' Itche Bartler from Kolomyja. In Zablotow he, with some partners leased the Profanation and was the bookkeeper and accountant. He and his wife were active in charities. He prayed at the Kosov synagogue. Following the death of R' Shmuel, at a young age, his wife remarried to R' Shnaryahu Meltzer who owned some properties. One of her grandsons arrived in Israel after going through the Holocaust in Europe and Cyprus.

R' Shimon Lindbaum, a scholar who owned a leather and shoe store, but later moved to Stanislavov to become a merchant. After the First World War his widow, his sons and his daughter returned to Zablotow to continue the leather business.

R' Shimon Altman was well versed in the words of our sages, followed the honest route. Owned a house not far from the tobacco factory where he made his living selling to the workers.

R' Shlomo Mechel Rosenshtock, a Chasid well versed in Jewish legends and Chasidic tales. Owned a house next to his brother-in-law R' Simcha Shochet who supported him. Was sick and died at a young age. Educated his children R' Mordechai Yisrael and R' David in Torah and the fear of God.

R' Shlomo Manches, was well versed in our righteous stories and an assistant to God in matchmaking. (was always in attendance when R' Aaron Keish lectured on Shabbos)

R' Shmaryahu Salpeter son of R' Shlomo the Gabay, was a Zionist scholar who knew how to sing.

R' Shaul Toyber was a scholar and fearful of God. Owned a small house on an alleyway and sold miscellaneous goods with his father, R' Aaron Yonah (brother of Rabbi Zalman Toyber) who was one of ten learned men of the synagogue of Kosov, first to enter and last to leave. Together with most of the Chasidim of Kosov he admired the Rabbis R' Yankele and his son R' Mendele.

R' Shmuel Toy was a respected man in town who daily learned a page of Gemara at the old synagogue where he prayed every day. Owned a white brick house and a general store where he traded with the farmers. Was a Kosher Jew keeping simple Jewish laws as well as more difficult ones. In his old age he emigrated with his wife Beila to Eretz Yisrael where they perished.

R' Davis Toy was a lumber merchant. Had a large house in the Market Square.

R' Tzvi Toy was a scholar who married a scholarly lady from Stanislavov. His business was banking. His wife, Fayke, excelled in her good qualities. Following his death she returned to her family in Stanislavov where she dedicated her life mainly to social issues and became well known for her good deeds. Their son David lives in Hertzlya, Israel.

Their son-in-law was **R' Yechiel Mechel Ernst** from a good family in Kosov who was a scholar, a Chasid and brought his sons up in Torah and general knowledge. Inherited his father-in-law's house and business

R' Anshel Ernest was an great scholar, R' David Klir's son-in-law who was a well-known merchant and an enthusiastic Chasid of the Rabbi of Otynya. Was a Gemara teacher for a while then immigrated to the United States. Later returned to Zablotow and died there. Educated his children in Torah and general knowledge.

Fishel is a Medical Doctor learned in New York.

R' Shmuel Toy son of Yoseph was a scholar who owned a house on the border between Demycze and Zablotow. Was considered among the richest and most respected men in town whose main business was agricultural product trading with the biggest property owners. On occasion he also acted as a broker in land deals. His son R' Moshe Hersh was a scholar who worked with his father. Later he left town and moved to Sziget to his father-in-law's house and lumber business. Natan was educated in general knowledge, moved to Vienna where he became a commercial trader. Wilhelm (Velvel) was educated in general knowledge, became a fire and life insurance agent. His sons-in-law R' Shmuel, R' Uri, and R' Moshe Greif were honest merchants. The forth son-in-law, R' Avraham Shrapshtein was the honest owner of a sawmill in Bukovina.

R' Shlomo Eizenberg a scholar married Gitel the daughter of R' Tzvi Rubin. His business was a grocery and general goods store serving the farmers. His son R' Abba and the other children were educated in Torah and business. His son-in-law R' Alexander Toy, son of Yakov Yoseph, was a Gabay at the Kosov synagogue. His son R' Tzvi Toy-Freid the first Holocaust survivor who reached our country, now lives in France.

III. Tradesman

Bakers

People in those days did not buy bread at the bakery since housewives had an oven in their homes and they baked bread, rolls and cakes for the whole week.

R' Meir Dunset had a large house in Demycze which he inherited from his father. His son Zev was a Hebrew teacher. Mechel was a baker like his father. Both left Zablotow to the United States. R' Meir drowned in the Pruth River one summer day.

R' Shalom Dunset owned a large house and a bakery oven on the street of the Main Synagogue. Was a well respected scholar, educated his children in Torah and general knowledge

R' David Zeiler baked dinner rolls etc. Educated his children to be honest.

Builders

All the houses in the city were built from lumber, the roofs from wooden shingles and the construction workers were mostly Jews who specialized in their profession. Only a few houses were built from stones or bricks.

R' Natan Fuchs and his sons R' Isaac the eldest, Moshe, Yakov, Avraham and Shabtay the youngest were all-powerful and excellent builders of wooden houses. R' Natan was a community politician and for a while a Gabay at the Main Synagogue as well as his sons R' Isaac and Avraham. They educated their children to follow in their profession.

R' Baruch Singer was a superb builder of wooden houses. An honest man who educated his children in Cheders and his profession.

R' Avraham Greif was a stone brick house-builder and a part time plasterer who excelled in profession and especially in building stoves. Was an honest man who educated his children in Torah.

R' Moshe Chaim who was lame was a constructor and a plasterer. Told long, descriptive stories. Was an excellent builder and plasterer of stoves. Educated his children in Torah. His son-in-law R' Berche was a Gemara teacher.

IV. Factories

The elders tell that they heard from their fathers that the tobacco factory in Demycze was built during the rule of Queen Maria Teresa after the partition of Poland and following the annexation of Eastern-Galicia and Bukovina to Austria. At the beginning it was a small factory. The farmers did not know how to grow the tobacco, but with the passing years the tobacco fields extended all the way from the Romanian border at one end and Podol'ye on the Russian border at the other. The small farmers as well as the large property owners found tobacco to be a well selling product. The factory developed into a large place with many clerks, guards, workers, storekeepers' etc. It was a self-governing empire with courts, jail, medical doctors, pharmacy, and armed guards in green uniforms and barrettes. Those guards had a unique duty to check all the farmers and make sure they brought all the produce to the factory during the harvest period (December to February) and did not keep any for themselves. Should they be caught with more then the permitted amount they were heavily fined or even jailed.

Following the harvest the farmers dried the tobacco and then sorted it and packaged it. (Each package contained 30 to 50 leaves). The tobacco was sold by weight while prices were determined in accordance with quality. Usually the farmers had a good income from growing tobacco.

There were no Jews in that "Government". All the personnel (workers, clerks etc.) were free of Jews. Following a long and tedious effort at the highest levels by the end of the last century, 50 young Jewish women were accepted, but had to leave soon after due to the hard working conditions which they were unaccustomed to. Jews had no place in the factory but indirectly largely benefited from it especially those living in Demycze next to the factory. It was a Jewish contractor who delivered all the material in and out of the factory and Jews were the suppliers of all lumber, boxes, sacks etc. All this was taken away from Jewish hands following the First World War when the Anti-Semite Polish took control over Zablotow. They established the "Kulka Ralintche" cooperative aimed at depriving food from all Jewish storekeepers and tradesmen causing great confusion in town and in the suburb of Demycze.

The first private linen factory was built by Mr. Yitschak Pistiner, R' Elezer Shtal's son-in-law from Kosov, who had great vision and commercial capabilities. He built the factory - a large two-story white-bricked building - next to the train station. Farmers were growing vast amounts of flax, agents were sent to buy it from them. Mr. Pistiner was not satisfied with just this factory, he dreamed of bigger things and sold it to R' Akiva Shreiber and his partner R' Aaron and his son Yehuda Rubin who kept the factory running for a few years. Mr. Pistiner moved to Lwow where he built a large shoe factory. Then, with some partners he rented a large sawmill and later he and a partner purchased a large property with a forest. He was unsuccessful in all of this, became entangled in some illegal matters and lost it all. This was the end of a man with great aspirations whose goal in life was to won large factories.

The single Post-Office in town belonged to a Polish man Yanitski. R' Moshe Shpilman, son of Berale the musician who was the mail deliveryman. He knew a bit of Polish and German and was ousted by the Polish after 40 years of service and immigrated with his family to the United States. Yanitski sold the post-office building to R' Yakov Veich who used it as a lumber warehouse.

V. Dayan

1. R' Zalman Toyber was the Dayan for Rabbi Yankele and Rabbi Mendele. He was a stocky stooped man fearful of God and well-versed in Torah. He was the only Dayan in town so he also served the Chasidim of R' Mendele from Demycze. He rose early to pray and to work at the synagogue of R' Yankele sitting till late judging cases and teaching (He taught a few youngsters for free). He had a sharp mind and was well conversed in worldly matters and even authored a book His son R' Meir was educated in Torah and to fear God. He inherited his father's house but not his wisdom and knowledge. He was an unsuccessful merchant. His only daughter, Miriam who was beautiful and smart, married R' Yechiel Chaim Kramer who was a well-known and successful merchant in Chernovtsy. He had a wholesale wine store known for its excellent wines and his honesty. They both were very active in charities, their home opened to the needy. They were barren.

2. R' Yeshayahu was accepted by Rabbi Mendele as a Dayan following R' Zalman's death. It was when the city split with the two Rabbi Dynasties to two separate communities, each with its own Dayan. R' Mendele from Demycze set up his Beth-Din (Jewish court) in his synagogue and so did the other community.

3. R' Shmeril Rotfeld was the first Jewish teacher at R' Mendele's community in Demycze. He was a scholar from Stanislavov, very well versed in Gemara and Halacha, who continued learning day and night, was very strict in his behavior and sang beautiful melodies during Shabbos and Holidays. His sons were all Torah scholars and feared God. R' Yeshayahu authored "Chazan Yeshayahu" but was an unsuccessful merchant. Later he became a Slaughterer in the village of Roznov. R' Wolf Itzik, his second son, a scholar and a merchant. R' Shmerel served Rabbi Mendele Hager and even his grandson R' Avraham Hager.

VI. Agriculture

A few important property owners lived in town. Some inherited the land while others leased them. Some had large fields of grain and tobacco. Some farmed the land together with their children from when it was plowed till harvest, but most used Gentile workers. It is a great mystery why young Jewish boys were not expected to do that work, had no other job and were sitting idle. There was always a shortage of farm workers. Property owners sent messengers all the way to the Karpathian Mountains in search of male and female workers. They came by droves on carriages, cut gathered and did all other necessary jobs for a few months and were paid nicely. The reasons given for not hiring the many Jewish workers are known; Jews are lazy, they did not have the skills required for these jobs, and one who hires a Jewish worker buys his own master. The Jewish youngsters had their own reason; its better to chase an easy job (or even be a beggar or thief) than work hard in agriculture. Fear of the Gentile workers did not help either, since there was a real danger of getting beaten by them. Those young lazy bums became successful pioneer farmers in Israel supporting their families and providing a great deal of produce to the citizens of the country.

R' Elyahu Reisher had a large house next to the train station where he had a grain barn and storage facilities for his produce. His son R' Yehuda inherited some of the land and continued in agriculture. R' Hillel Goldshtein, his son-in-law, inherited some of the fields and farmed them and traded in grain. He purchased the Mimlis house from Frankel who was Mimlis's son-in-law after the authorities invoked his licenses. The Reisher family was honest, especially R' Hillel Goldshtein.

R' Yakov Loib, son-in-law of R' Yehoshua Toy son of Mordechai, owned a large house in Demycze including place to store the harvest, horses and tools. His sons R' Itzik and Moshe were educated in Torah and helped their father.

The old R' Mordechai Toy was engaged in farming and in religious matters. He was a Gabay in the old synagogue and was busy learning Torah all the times. Was among the early risers and the last to leave, easily angered and very strict. It was virtually impossible to get a candle from him to be able to learn at night. His son R' Neta Toy who was stocky man inherited his house and property. His only son, R' Catriel worked with his father, later inherited from him. They had a large house in the Market Square with a barn and storage room for their grain. He was a partner in the ferry on the Pruth River for a short time.

R' Moshe Tzvi Greif inherited his land. He had a large house at the front of the Market Square and at the back a corridor facing the synagogues with storage room and a horse stable. He used to place his trash in the back across from the neighbors and the synagogues, causing bad odors, flies and rats. He educated his children in Cheders. He was a partner in the ferry on the Pruth River for a short time. His son, Yechiel Greif was a scholar always learning Torah like his brothers Yehoshua and Baruch. He feared the Army and afflicted himself until he died a single man. It is rumored that he died of Pneumonia like his mother and brother Yehoshua. Baruch Greif immigrated to the United States and later brought his father over. R' Yakov Yoseph Toy was R' Moshe's (above) brother. Had a large house in Demycze and properties managed by him and his sons. R' Leib and the other sons were all farmers and horse owners. Rivka and Reuven are Holocaust refugees and are in Israel. Reuven left Israel and immigrated to Canada following false accusations that he corroborated with the Nazis in Zablotow and Kolomyja.

R' Shmuel Troschenitzer owned a large house and a tool shed. His sons Isaac and Tzvi were educated in Cheders and helped him in his work. The house was sold to R' Moshe Gutartz.

R' Shmuel Libber was always learning Gemara. He had a large house with a barn and storerooms for all the grain collected from his fields, which were leased, to Gentile farmers. Was well respected in the community and prayed in the Kosov synagogue. His son R' Moshe Libber was a scholar who later inherited the house and properties. He educated his children in Torah, was a Chasid and, like his father, gave generously to charities. Pessi, his only daughter, married R' Zev (Velvele) Heinish from Kolomyja whose parents were scholars and learned Torah. R' Zev was a great scholar, he did not work and concentrated on his learning at the Kosov's synagogue all day. He taught some boys for free and during many long nights wrote notes, which he hoped to publish, however they were lost. (How pitiful). He was destined to be a great Rabbi some day but he died young survived by his young wife and two orphans. His son Meir was brought up by his mother Pessi, in Cheder, in Torah and fear of God. He was very smart, excelled in Torah and Jewish studies and had a great future ahead of him. During that time many youngsters were caught up in the Jewish Zionist National movements, and so did the young, genius Meir. He became a very active Zionist and a perfect Hebrew writer whose articles and descriptions of Jewish Life were published all around Galicia. He lived in Kolomyja were he worked as a bookkeeper and an accountant, later he moved to Stanislavov, where he was the manager of the Zionist bank and the editor of the paper "The Jew". He was a soldier during the First World War and then lived in Vienna where he was the manager of the Joint Bank, editor and publisher of important Hebrew, Yiddish and German papers. He was one

of the founders of the "Cooperative" in Austria and among the most active
in the Zionist Federation. Today he lives in Tel-Aviv, Israel.

VII. Chazan

R' Zelig Dresner was the chief Chazan in town, mainly performing Jewish weddings, chanting "Me Sheberach" etc. and was the Chazan in the Main Synagogue during Shabbos and Holidays. He was also the "Shamash" at the old synagogue for which he obtained a narrow room and a small kitchen. He lived all his life in poverty and had two sons, one became a porter, the other a tutor (teacher's assistant).

R' Shalom Fuchs inherited R' Zelig's position. He was the son-in-law of the famous and rich R' Moshe Alter, who chose R' Shalom for his only daughter, Esther, who was a very gentle, fine, delicate, cultured, educated and smart woman. R' Shalom had a soft and pleasant voice and an excellent Chazan during the High Holidays. During the life of R' Moshe they enjoyed the good life and respect of the community. A special respect was bestowed on him in the Kosov Synagogue where people enjoyed his prayers during Shabbos and Holidays, but as soon as R' Moshe died everything turned sour. He had to sell the house they inherited at a loss and the money he obtained ran out in a very short time. He was then given old R' Zelig's position and with the "honor" of being a beggar. To make his condition even worse, Esther was sick and became paralyzed while he lost his eyesight. They both died young in these miserable conditions.

VIII. Other Professions As Sources of Income

Men's Tailors

R' Aaron, son of Risia, was a tall man, a tenant of R' Efrayim Fond. Educated his children in Torah and to continue in his profession. A group of tailors charged high prices with the excuse of donating it to the needy including the old R' Zalman Aaron, R' Aaron Funi, R' Shalom and his sons R' Hersh and R' Shechna.

Women's Tailors

R' Mendele Shteiner who knew some writing and reading, was for a while a Gabay at the synagogue of Tailors and Craftsmen which was next to the Main Synagogue, and he was the Chairman of the society of Women's Tailors.

Sources of Income

There were a few opportunities for a good income, which provided work, and livelihood for the town. Among them were:

The Tuesday Market brought in farmers from the area who sold their produce and their cattle, and in return purchased goods. Special Markets were held four to six times a year, especially the "Holoviski" Markets, which lasted three days (during the beginning of the fall - in Ellul). Hundreds of groups brought in their fattened cattle from the Karpathian Mountains. There were Cattle ranchers and dealers from the entire country selling and buying cattle and horses. From here they were sent to the markets of Vienna and Berlin. Camps for the cattle and horses were established in town but mostly in the area between the Pruth River and the canal.

The Tobacco Factory generated a lot of money. Hundreds, sometimes even a thousand, people worked there, especially during harvest time (December to February) when up to a hundred carriages arrived daily with their produce all the way from Bukovina, Podol'ye, the Karpathian Mountains etc. They stayed in town up to 10 days following their trade at the factory/

In those days, carriages and wagons were the only means of transportation, since the trains had not yet been fully developed, and the prices were considered high. This required places to room and board for the people associated with this industry; dealers, merchants, drivers' etc. Thus, Jews were the providers of these needs. They were the purchasing agents, buyers, moneylenders (Gentiles borrowed money almost every day) and Jews provided the farmers with their household goods. Jews were happy with their side of the bargain and the Gentiles with the good service provided. Good relations existed between the Jews and the Ukrainians; there were very few Poles in the area, Gentiles did not hurt the Jews and the Kolkaralnitchi organization and the others were created later.

Taverns and Bars

R' Zev Rosenboim one of town respected elders, had a large house in Demycze including a yard with rooms for carriages and horses, an inn and a restaurant next to the tobacco factory. He educated his sons in Cheders. His eldest son, R' Mordechai Yo'el had a large house and a bank which brought disaster. R' Shmuel Nathan owned properties. His other sons had houses and were grain dealers. His only daughter was nice looking, smart, cultured, knew how to read and write and married (second marriage) David, son of R' A.L. Shfarber.

R' Chaim Toy son of Yoseph owned a large house and a yard next to Rabbi Yenkele. He had a hotel, a tavern and a restaurant where many Chasidim stayed while visiting Rabbi Yenkele. He was a scholar and prayed in R' Yankele synagogue. R' Netta Toy died young. R' Yankele Toy married R' Hersch Herman's daughter. The whole family perished during the Holocaust.

Brothers R' Yonah and Shimon Singer had a large house with room for carriages, horses etc. which provided them with a limited income. They sold the house to the government that built the courthouse there and the large two-story jail. They educated their children in Torah. R' Yonah was a scholar and walked every Shabbos to the old synagogue to hear a lecture despite the long distance from his house.

R' Yecheskel Reisher owned a few properties and fields leased to Gentiles, and a large house in Demycze with space for carriages, a hotel and a restaurant for intellectuals, and a wine house where his beautiful wife, Riva-Necha served them. His guests included most of the property owners, clerks from the tobacco factory and the town's intellectuals. She was the daughter of the strict Gabay R' Mordechai Toy. She was barren, and the inheritance was shared between the Toy and Resher families.

R' Yitzchak (Isaac) Oyerbach was a well-respected and presentable man with a large house next to the Pravoslavic Church. His house, which included room for carriages and horses, a hotel, a restaurant visited by most of the important guests in town, and a tavern for the Gentiles. Educated his sons in Torah and general knowledge. His son R' Moshe was a scholar who married a rich woman from Bukovina. He lived in his father-in-law's house and was successful. R' Arche was not a scholar (except for a well-known game), but following his marriage with a rich woman from Poitela he succeeded in his trade and became well respected in that town. The youngest son, Menachem (Mendy) a young scholar died at a young age.

R' Yehoshua Toy owned a large house with a hotel and a restaurant next to the Kosov's synagogue. His only son, R' Alter inherited the house and the business and added a Butcher store. His son Eliyahu who was R' Aaron Rubin's son-in-law, was a scholar, a smart and capable man. He inherited the comfortable house which included a nice ballroom for weddings, dances and, as well as meetings and public lectures.

Brothers R' Yisrael and R' Moshe Frost were well-respected scholars who had a large house with a wide alley between the houses. Both houses included hotels and taverns. Both of them prayed in the Main Synagogue and served as Gabays there. R' Elchanan, R' Moshe's eldest son, was a scholar who married a rich woman from Kosmatch in the Karpathian Mountains and joined his father-in-law's business. The second son, R' Leib inherited the house and business but was unsuccessful and lost it all. R' Yisrael's eldest son, R' Elchanan, was a scholar and a grain merchant in his father's house. The second son, R' Yakov opened a successful grocery store in his father's house. His two sons were the town's newspaper agents and distributors during the years between the two world wars.

R' Yisrael Ashpil one of the most respected men in town had a large house in the corner facing the south side of the market square and the road to Gevozdets on the east side. The house, which included a hotel, restaurant, tavern, and room for carriages, was bustling with traffic coming and going, day and night. R' Yehoshua Milich, his son-in-law inherited the house and lived there comfortably, till it burnt down in 1880 or 1881 a fire that destroyed the whole street. R' Yehoshua sold the lot to R' David Toy son of R' Shmuel and moved back to his birth-town of Podheitz. R' David Toy built a two story stone and brick house with a tin roof (it was the first such building in town). He rented the house to the government for ten years. It served as the local courthouse, land registry, customs and a jail at the back just across from the synagogue. People did not appreciate that fact and resented him for desecrating the place. A few years later he became very sick and he died on the operating table in a hospital in Lwow. People considered his death to be his punishment for the desecration.

R' Catriel Weiss from Bukovina, R' Elkana Kugler's son-in-law, inherited his house in the town center, with a linen, wool and silk store. It was unsuccessful and he opened a tavern and a restaurant for Jewish travelers. Later he left town and moved to a farm, which was his inheritance. He was even tempered, a scholar, well-liked and active in charities. The house and restaurant were sold to R' Tzvi Hersch (Hersh Leib) Fishel son of Yonah, who made it prosperous.

R' Pinchas (Pini) Waller a scholar whose wife Cherna was R' Chaim Zimel Singer's sister. He owned a large house, a cellar, a tavern and a large yard next to the train station. The tavern was always full. R' Isaac, his eldest son, was educated in Cheders, owned a house next to his father's, had some property and sold cattle. R' Leib, one of R' Isaac's sons, was one of the wealthiest men in town during the two world wars. He served for a while as the head of the community and as Deputy Mayor. He was captured by the Russians during the Second World War and died on his way there. His wife and one son somehow survived somewhere in Russia. R' David had a farm in Davlovitch R' Leib (len) graduated as a Lawyer from the Polish College and opened a practice in Kolomyja. R' Gershon inherited the house and the business, and educated his sons in general knowledge. R' Chaim Leib Lester was one of his grandsons. He was a literate scholar who immigrated to the United States.

Brothers R' Pinchas and R' Meir Haber were grandsons of R' Moshe Yehuda Karsel. They purchased the Large courthouse and Jail from R' David Toy. The wheel of fortune is turning, and they were successful in their trade and able to purchase that property and turn it back into a hotel and a restaurant. They developed a very good reputation for serving the best food and drinks, and passengers filled the place at all times providing the owners with a steady profit. They lived like traditional Kosov Chasidim, supported their parents and gave them a large home and a store of their own.

Midwife

Chaya Rachel Singer was the only midwife in town. Her husband was R' Mordechai Singer who was a simple Jew, and for a short time served as a supervisor of the farm workers at some of the large properties. Their son Yakov was a carriage driver.

Teachers

R' Avraham Sheinhorn became a teacher following his unsuccessful bid in business. From his father R' Meir Eliezer he inherited half a house with an alley for horses and carriages and obtained the hotel which provided his livelihood. He was well respected and had great knowledge in Gemara which he shared with some young boys. He educated his children in Torah and general knowledge.

R' Aaron Helper became a teacher by chance, was a Chasid of Kosov, feared God and taught Gemara and Torah and Jewish ethics. He educated his children in Torah and fear of God.

R' Binyamin Yisrael Rosenboim the son of the tinsmith R' David was a professional teacher. He was a scholar who read the Torah beautifully and taught Gemara, Torah and Torah reading. He was a Chasid of Chortkov and he educated his children in Torah and general knowledge.

R' Yitzchak (nicknamed Itzekel Footerel) was a teacher from a young age who taught Gemara and Torah. His wife sold household items, toys, poultry and eggs in the market.

R' Moshe Baruch Hirsch became a teacher by chance and later left town.

R' Elkana the 'tall man', R' Dov (Berel, blind in one eye), R' Meir and R' Shoel taught the Alpha-Bet, pronunciation, Torah reading, Rashi letters, and Torah for ages three to six. Each of them had a teaching assistant and taught thirty to forty children in a narrow dark Cheder (room) with no air or light.

R' Berel had a large house next to the public-bath- house with three large rooms and a four by four meters area where he had about forty boys and girls. His assistant taught about forty more children in the other room. The third room had a kitchen where his wife and daughter prepared food in addition to working in the yard taking care of a cow and a carriage. The children played outside during the summer days next to the pond, which was full of frogs, reptiles and insects, but during the winter they slid on the frozen water.

R' Zev (Velvel) Dunest was teaching up to ten boys Torah, Rashi, Gemara, arithmetic, Yiddish and a little Hebrew. His wife Sheva had a grocery store in the market where their sons Yoseph and Zalman worked as well. Yoseph immigrated to the United States. Zalman Dunest owns a house in the City Square and a Soda water factory. Moshe Dunest his son was very talented and became the top Communist in town. R' Reuven Dunest, R' Zev's brother, taught Torah, Gemara, arithmetic, Yiddish and German. He was well accepted and became familiar with worldly knowledge.

R' Moshe Mendel Gadels was blind in one eye, and taught Torah, Rashi, Gemara, Yiddish and a little Hebrew. He was a Chazan in the Kosov synagogue on Shabbos. His wife sold eggs, vegetables, chickens etc. from her house.

R' Feibish Feiger taught Torah, Rashi, Mishna and Gemara at homes of his students. He was a very good Chazan during Shabbos and Holidays and prayed at nearby farms, usually for a salary. N. Feiger, his son, moved to Stanislavov and became the Chazan at the synagogue of the intellectuals.

R' Shimon Hirsh was a storekeeper for a while, later he became a teacher of Mishna and Gemara for older boys. Was an enthusiastic Chasid of Viznica and Otynya.

R' Avraham Gross was a great scholar, a Zionist well versed in literature and general education. He taught Gemara, Torah and grammar. He educated his pupils in the Zionist spirit and participated many times in the Mizrachi meetings in Lwow, emigrated with his family to Eretz Yisrael in 1923. For many years he worked as a bookbinder and now he is a sick man. Rivka his daughter is a teacher in Ein-Charod. Shulamit his second daughter and his son are living in Tel-Aviv.

R' Binyamin Gross, a brother of R' Avraham, was a bookbinder as well and an enthusiastic Zionist did not managed to emigrate to Eretz Yisrael but perished with his entire family during the Holocaust

Clerks

R' Elchanan Shtachel was a modest scholar and a Chasid. He composed claims and requests to the courts, edited contracts etc. His only son was educated in Torah and general knowledge. His grandson lives in Israel.

R' Tzvi, nicknamed bald Hirsch was an excellent clerk, a scholar, and owned a large house and an office. He educated his children in Torah and general knowledge. Most of the language teachers were clerks as well.

Musicians

One group of musicians was well liked in town. They were simple, uneducated, poor and hardly made a living.

R' Berele Shpilman played the long violin, was the conductor and good at his profession. His son Moshe followed in his footsteps as a good violinist. He later became a post-man for forty years. He was a simple man who hardly knew how to read. He was ousted from his post by the Polish and immigrated to the United States.

Yehuda Izy was a flute player. Elyahu played the piano. Meir was the drummer. Another played the cymbal while still another the castanets.

Each was very good with his instrument despite not being students of any music conservatory. They played at weddings in town, at the property owner's homes, outlying villages, during holidays, Chanukah, Purim, the end of Yom Kippur etc. They were very well liked in town and it is hard to imagine a Jewish wedding without Berele and his band.

Long ago being a musician was considered long ago to be an important and holy Jewish profession, but not so in Zablotow where it became a contemptible job like many others. (One who wished to look down at or tease another used to call him: tailor, shoemaker or musician etc.) It is true that most (but not all) of the artisans were uneducated especially the musicians with some of them deteriorated like Feibish, Berele's son, who became a thief and a robber.

His father educated him as a musician, but after a short time he left his father and the music, organized a group of pickpockets who 'graduated' to become thieves. He was the leader of the pack, was caught a few times, and sentenced first to serve a few months and later a few years. Lately he's been caught in a hard crimes (robbery or murder) and sentenced to twenty years in jail with hard labor on an isolated island where he died. (It is rumored that he and one of his cohorts managed to escape through a crack in the wall and disappeared).

Language Teachers

N. Greminger was a school graduate and taught German, Polish and arithmetic privately by the hour. Zev (Velvel) Toy , Ranche's son was a scholar with a sharp mind who taught German. Especially the youngsters accepted him in town. He was a clerk, as well and died a bachelor. Tzvi (Hirsch) Reiter, son of Berel the shoemaker, taught Polish, Ukrainian, and arithmetic. He was a clerk, as well who prepared requests etc. Tzvi Toy (Hirsch Prince) became a German and arithmetic teacher, later immigrated with his family to the United States. (He was R' Mordechai Fisher's son-in-law). Shlomo Zalman Zeiler was a student but did not a graduate of the Music School. He taught Polish and Ukrainian and was a clerk, as well.

Carpenters

R' Avraham Gloger was an expert carpenter, an honest man, involved in community work and was for a short time the Gabay at the Synagogue of the Craftsmen. Meir Yakov, His son-in-law was craftsman who specialized in doors and windows, and owned his own home

R' Avraham Cholem had a large house with room for horses next to the synagogue.

R' Berche Kelbali (a tease or his family name?) and his brother-in-law R' Tzvi were expert carpenters and honest. Berche had a house next to the market, while Tzvi had his near the Pruth River.

Lawyer

The first Zablotow lawyer Herman Shapira had an aura about him, he assimilated and knew no Hebrew or Jewish reading. He purchased R' Ovadya Greif's house renovated it into a large office and added a nice flower garden. He educated his sons to assimilate among the Gentiles and have no contact with Jews.

Salesladies

There were about a dozen women who had booths at the market. A booth had four poles, two meters by two meters, and two meters high as well. On three sides there were linen sheets or wooden planks, while the top had a roof against the rain. There was half a meter between adjacent booths. They used the booths daily for selling their merchandise consisting of household items and children toys.

Blima the widow was one of the main Salesladies. She was the widow of R' Shmuel son of R' Avraham Yakov who owned the Profanation. She had all the good qualities required for being successful; gossipy, jealousy etc. arguing with customers, shouting at her neighbor for allowing her customers to step into her space, her loud voice was heard for miles.

The second was Patelitche, wife of Avram Potelinski, was very similar to Blima, her neighbor if not exactly like her.

The third was Miriam Yassi (Mariassi) wife of R' Mendel Tshantchik. She was a modest woman who prayed daily in the synagogue with the Minyan (A group of at least ten men) and used to recite Tehilim (Book of Psalms) when she had no customers. She donated generously to charity and educated her sons in Torah and the fear of God.

The fourth etc, were all similar to the first and second.

On the other side of the market was the fruit area. One of the women there was the wife of Yacov (Yacov Yechchi) Halfenbein who visited his own home twice a year for Passover and for the High Holidays. All year round he traveled from town to town, village to village in Galicia and Bukovina. What was he doing there? It is rumored that he was a beggar pretending to be a grandson of some famous Rabbi. He had the ability to mix in his regular conversation with verses from the Bible even drunk, after drinking 96 proof whiskey. His audience was simple people who donated a little, but one by one it added up.

On the third side of the market stood women selling fresh vegetables and produce that they brought daily from the farms, especially on Tuesdays. Thus the "Women's Market' was in the shape of a U.

Authors

R' Gershon was an expert scribe (for Torah Tfilin and Mezuza) and for divorce papers (Gett) etc. He was an honest and a modest man who worked out of his small house.

R' David lived in Kolomyja and came to Zablotow occasionally to sell his merchandise and get a few orders. He moved to Zablotow following R' Gershon's death.

Barbers

R' Aaron was a physician and a barber. His wife as well was children barber. His brother-in-law David Hirsh and another man from Demycze were sort of physicians: they bandaged wounds, drew blood, used leeches, pulled out teeth etc.

Horse traders

R' Chaim Meir Zeiler was an honest chubby man who owned a large house next to Rabbi Yankele's, who he admired and prayed in his synagogue. R' Moshe, his son, inherited the house and business, had an inclination towards higher education and sent one son to Kolomyja. Shlomo Zalman was educated in Kolomyja in general education. He was an honest man. R' David was a horse trader first, later became a baker. R' Nisan was a general merchant, later moved to Kolomyja and opened a grocery store. They were all honest men.

Carters

1. R' Zeide Toy who owned a one horse carriage was the first to carry people to and from the train station in the days when trains were not yet common and still expensive. Only the wealthy used the train and R' Zeide's wagon, while most walked on foot. Over the years prices decreased causing an increase in train transportation and thus more carriages and two-horse wagons. They provided transportation to nearby towns such as Kosov, Kuty, Viznica, etc.

2. Chana Cholem, R' Yehuda Hersch Oyerbach's son-in-law, had a two horse wagon.

3. Yoseph Eizenkraft was first a merchant, then later had a two-horse wagon. During the years between the wars he and his wife Riva had a popular restaurant. In 1942 he committed suicide so as not to be killed by the Nazis when they came to take him away. His family perished in the Holocaust except for one son Tzvi who emigrated with his family to Israel where he is working as a steelworker.

4. Yakov Singer, son of Rachel the midwife, had a two-horse carriage.

5. Alter Maltchek had a two-horse carriage, became blind in his old age. His son Chaim is in Israel.

6. Eliezer Fuchs, a grandson of R' Avraham Yacov (his father died at a young age) had a one horse wagon with which he shuttled up to twelve passengers to and from Kolomyja.

7. Aaron, his brother had a one-horse carriage, as well. He was a bachelor.

8. Their brother-in-law, R' Fishel had a one horse carriage serving the Kolomyja route. He was an honest man.

Besides getting paid for transporting people, the carriage owners had an income from serving as buyers for the small storekeepers.

9. R' Tzvi (Hirsch Yehuda Moshe's) owned a two horse carriage suitable for up to fifteen passengers. His route was Sniatin which, was the District Capital with its government offices and tax center (which was lacking in Zablotow). Like his fellow tradesmen, he bought merchandise in Sniatin for storekeeper in Zablotow. His house, which included a yard

for his horses and carriage, was located immediately next to the old synagogue. The people praying there and in the other neighboring synagogues did not like it at all since his carriage was always standing in their way in front of his house and the smell from his horses filled the air. He educated his sons to be tailors. They immigrated to the United States following their service in the Army. Moshe Bahn (nicknamed Bahn for his fast horse that ran as fast as the train called Bahn) was married to his only daughter. Following R' Tzvi's death he inherited the house and the Sniatin route.

Load Carrying Carters

R' Alter Manis, was an honest man educating his sons in Torah. His son R' Yitzchak learned all day, he had a small grocery store. Hirsh Manis had a two-horse wagon for carrying load, like his father's.

R' Shabtay Shterenberg who was a grain dealer owned a house next to the Pruth river. His wife sold flour and eggs out of the house. She was famous for her quality flour. His son R' Elezer Shterenberg was a grain dealer at first, later owned a two horse wagon. R' Shabtay Avraham, Mechel and Tzvi were educated in Torah and were grain dealers.

R' Feibel Bercher the Cohen had a house and owned Carriages. His sons Leib, Yoel and Mooki had carriages as well. Mooki was the head of the Carter's in Zablotow, he was a strong man but a gentle Jew, honest and kind.

R' David Adlershtein had a carriage for carrying loads and later became a successful grain dealer. He had a large house, was a Kosov Chasid and educated his sons in Torah and general knowledge.

R' Yacov Leib Adlershtein, his brother, also owned a carriage then later became a successful merchant and owner of a large house.

R' Moshe (Avramel's) Toy had a two horse wagon. He and his wife Esther, donated to charity, were hospitable during weekdays and Shabbos, wrote a Torah scroll and donated it to the Kosov synagogue. They had no children.

Tinsmiths

R' David Rosenboim was a pious Jew, a Chasid of the Rabbi from Chortkov, fast in his work and in his prayers. He educated his sons in Torah and the fear of God. R' Yacov Mechel his son, learned Gemara and Torah, moved to his father-in-law's house in Horodenka where he had a store. His two son-in-laws were important merchants and well versed in Torah.

R' Iser son of R' Avraham Gloger had a tinsmith shop next to R' David Rosenboim.

Butchers

Most of them lived in town, the others in Demycze, each had a house and a butcher store. They were all honest and strict and they were not suspected of selling non-Kosher meat.

- R' Avraham and his brother R' Mordechai (Mooki) Fishel sons of Beile Rissi.
- R' Efrayim Alya and his son R' Tzvi and his son-in-law. His grandson was a scholar, he moved to Kolomyja where he had a wood heating business.
- R' Zelig Shafer.
- R' Yehoshua Fishel.
- R' Leib Libber son of Leah.
- R' Shmuel Libber son of Leah had properties leased to Gentiles.
- R' Mechel Sheiner and his son R' David who immigrated later to the United States. Zeide a second son was a live fish dealer.
- R' Kalman Shfarber and his sons Abba and Feivel who later became merchants.
- R' Shamay Shafer and his son Kalman who later moved to his father-in-law in Viznica.

Rope Makers

R' Yehoshua Burg and his sons Zeide and Yoseph. He had a house in the alley where he made his ropes outside during the summer. His sons Zeide and Yoseph left this horrible work to become traveling merchants.

R' Shlomo Grayer or Graber was the second to have this profession together with his son Gabriel. They had a large house in which they later built a successful press for various products.

Physicians

Dr. N. Heren was the first and only doctor in town. He was assimilated and had no connection with the Jewish spirit. Dr. Kalir before him was an experienced doctor, a Catholic and well liked.

Following his death a young physician came to town, Dr. N. Neinberg who was a proud Zionist Jew who became a crowd favorite. Later he moved to Chernovtsy to be a City Doctor where he became famous for his Zionist activities.

Saddlers

R' Aaron Reiter and his son Itche were honest men, they had a house next to R' Chaim Karsel. Buzi one of Itche's sons escaped the killings of Zablotow and is living in Tel-Aviv, Israel making a living as a tailor.

R' Dov Reiter and his sons were expert saddlers. Mordechai was the buyer of raw material while Tzvi Leib was a college student

R' Eliezer Burg bought the raw material. His sons did the work. Others were: His brother Berel Burg, Davis Periliss, Chane Pupik and Chaim Benish's, all were honest men who worked from their house, and prayed at the small artisans' synagogue.

Slaughterers and Examiners

R' Simcha Shechter was an honest man, a scholar who was always clean both on the outside and the inside. He was a descendant of a well-respected family. His house was on the border with Demycze where he always had out of town guests. He supplied them with room and board so he never ate breakfast or lunch alone. He supported local charities as well and assisted his family and the needy emptying his pockets by nightfall. Occasionally, when he could not afford it, he borrowed large sums of money so as to be able to give to others, and when necessary he approached other wealthy men to help him.

Simcha Shechter's only son R' Mordecha'le inherited not only his father's house but his good qualities and behavior and charity, as well. He educated his four sons in Torah and general education but hey did not want to be slaughterers. R' Meshulam was a scholar, at first he dealt in wood for heating then later he became a bookkeeper and accountant for the largest mill in Storozinec. During the First War World he immigrated to Vienna where he became a merchant. He died young. Yehoshua was a merchant, later he immigrated to the United States. Yakov Shimshon. Simcha Gershon, R' Mordechale's son-in-law, had a sharp mind, was a great scholar, well versed in Torah and Gemara and became a rabbi in some city, later in Bukovina.

R' Davis Tzvi Gross was R' Simcha's first son-in-law. He was a scholar both in Torah and in Jewish textbooks. He taught boys at his house for free. He educated his sons In Torah and general education. R' Zelig his son was a scholar and one of the founders of the Zionist movement in Zablotow. Toni (Yonah) his daughter immigrated to Israel and is living with her husband Yoseph Kuperman and their son in Haifa.

R' Simcha's second son-in-law was R' Yisrael Freidfertig, son of R' Avraham Oslover. He was a scholar and owned a house and saw mill in Oslov not far from Delyatin. His son-in-law was, R' Baruch Haber, a wood dealer in Mikulichin. He was R' Moshe Yehuda Karsel's grandson. Zelig, his son, immigrated to Israel a few years ago and was killed in Haifa on duty serving his country and the people in the "Hagana", on the first day of Adar A' 1948.

Judges

The only Jewish Judge was N. Sochbor in the town of Naduvrena. He and his family assimilated in order to obtain the post of a chairman and moved to Zablotow to become the Chief Justice. He paraded in all the

Holidays with his family and the priests. There were four judges in the court, and Jews and Gentiles alike hated him.

Shamash (Maintenance)

- R' Yacov (Yukov) whose family name was not known maybe and perhaps even to himself, was the city and the main synagogue's Shamash. He completed all his duties by sunrise, starting sometimes as early as three AM. He woke Jews up to their morning prayers by knocking with his hammer on their doors and windows. On Friday afternoons he walked around town knocking with his hammer on stores telling Jews the time of the start of Shabbos. On Shabbos he made all the announcements on behalf of the authorities. He took care of all the weddings, circumcisions, Bar-Mitzvahs etc. and was reworded handsomely for that and on Holidays, Chanukah, Purim etc.
- R' Binyamin inherited R' Yucov's position following his death, and was very much like him in all respects.
- R' Mordechai Mooki Lachtermacher (meaning; fixing the lamps. Was it his name or his profession) was the second Shamash dedicated to handling burials. He was the one who confirmed a death by placing a light feather on the person's mouth. He made the coffins at the old synagogue where people prayed six or seven times a day, maybe to remind them where they came from and what their destiny is. During funerals he held a charity plate yelling "Rightness before God". He covered the deceased's eyes with the broken pottery. Following the burial he gathered the mourners for their first meal and whisky. Throughout his entire life R' Mooki was efficient at what he did both privately and publicly. He lived with his family in the cemetery. His assistant, the gravedigger, only did what R' Mooki told him to do.

IV. Farms and Villages that were part of the town

Il'intse

R' Baruch (Avremel's) Toy lived here. He was an honest man who worked for the Christian village owner who found that R' Baruch performs his duties well. His son Tzvi and two sisters immigrated to our land and are taking part in its resurrection.

R' Menachem Holder was a pious Jew who studied Torah most of the time and was employed at the local tavern. His son R' Moshe David Holder was a scholar who moved to his father-in-law in Kalush where he became a successful merchant of wood and forests. Later he built a large sawmill producing planks, which he exported. He had a large house in Stanislavov. His five sons all worked in the business and became rich. They were educated in Torah and business.

Oleshkov

R' Moshe Shfarber leased a large property. He was a Kosov Chasid, very hospitable and worked in charities. He donated land with a house to the Kosov synagogue where his brother, R' Tzvi Avraham Shfarber lived all his life. Following his death the house was given to the synagogue. He educated his sons in Torah and general knowledge. His sons Efrayim and Feivel leased land and were very much like their father. His son Yehoshua was Rabbi R' Azri'el's son-in-law from Yablonov (Steptesht). He died very young. Another son, R' Natan Shfarber was a scholar. He leased a Lime and Cement factory in the District of Stanislavov. He acted like a Chasid and gave to charities. A few years later he immigrated to Germany where he built a successful Sacks Factory, was well-respected in town and contributed to the community. He educated his sons well and they were well mannered. R' Avraham David Reisenberg leased the property which was vacated by R' Moshe Shfarber. His son-in-law, R' Mordechai Koren, was a wealthy man, contributed to the community, always protected the Governors, was a grain merchant with his father-in-law and was chairman of the community for a while. His son Berche was the sole survivor of the Holocaust.

Areletse

R' Elyahu Shtadler knew Torah well, was an old and pleasant man, well respected, had some land which was taken cared by his sons. His grandson, R' Abba, was a scholar, married the daughter of R' Zelig Chalibitchner and moved to live with him. Second grandson, R' Nachum Shtadler, had a sharp mind and a very good memory. He was a teacher for a while, and after his marriage he graduated from Teacher's College and was a teacher in The Baron Hirsh Jewish School in Kozolov and later in Tarnopol. He was a good teacher, well respected, an enthusiastic Zionist who was great speaker. Speaking at the Main Synagogue in front of thousands, he became so emotional that he became ill and died at a young age leaving a young widow and two young daughters. His widow and his two daughters immigrated to Israel where one of them, Yael, is active in the community as she was in Zablotow.

R' Eliezer Shtadler, was a pious Jew, a Visnica Chasid, a scholar who owned some properties which provided him with an income. He educated his sons in Torah, in the town. His son R' Moshe was a scholar, a farmer and later a lumber merchant in Sadagura.

Gan'kovtsy

R' Shimon Hipsher, a scholar and property owner. His son, Yecheskel (Karl) was college educated and became the town's secretary following his graduation. He was respected by the authorities in Sniatin who accepted most of his actions, which benefited the citizens. He served for over forty years in this position working for the Gentile Mayor and the Anti-Semitic City Councilors.

Voysekhovitse

R' Chaim who was called Chaim Voysekhovitser was an honorable scholar who had some properties and a large house with a store and a tavern. Most of the local villagers were his customers and they used to sit in his tavern and have whiskey and drinks. He had a nice-looking virgin daughter who was engaged to Pesach Toy son of R' Moshe Zanvil. At the same time, a young Gentile was among those drinking dailies at the tavern. He eyed the beautiful girl and somehow managed to persuade her to join him. He smuggled her out of the house one night, brought her to a priest who sent her to a convent in Sniatin where, after a few days she converted.

One Saturday in August 1877 there was a parade where hundreds of priests, men women and children marched through Zablotow to celebrate their Holiday with their idols. A Jewish man passing on the street (this was unusual as Jews stayed away during these parades) noticed R' Chaim Voysekhovitser's daughter in the crowd. He immediately told it to his friends, Natan Fuchs's strong sons who got some more of their friends and they decided to get her out and save her from Christianity. Later that night while the young Gentiles where dancing in front of the Church they kidnapped the young girl and ran away with her. It was not yet the time for (the Verse to Happen):" Five of you will chase a hundred, and a hundred will chase ten-thousands", they miscalculated the situation. There were a few thugs amongst the Gentiles who chased our boys, caught them and rescued the girl. All the young Gentiles heard what had happened and went out to the streets and started hitting every Jew they met, thus started a riot where stores fronts were broken, and stores ransacked. The police were called in, dressed in their uniforms and feathered hats, armed with swords and frightening rifles, and the night guards - about thirty men all together - and they managed to stop the raging animals.

Thirty men could not prevent the hundreds from continuing their rampage of destruction if not for the All Mighty in the sky. A strong storm brewed breaking trees, destroying rooftops, raising sand and dust from the river banks and blinding people. The skies darkened, lightning flashed, thunder rumbled and horrific rain and hail poured down. The mob panicked thinking God had intervened and fled out of town by foot or by horse carriages. A short time later there was no sign of them.

Jews kept a vigil all that night, keeping all doors, windows and shutters locked, and staying indoors. News about the incident spread and many people came in to see and hear what had happened. The case reached the courts, and a few boys were charged but the judge acquitted them for lack of evident (court judges treated the citizens fondly and were strongly influenced by the Mayor who asked them to treat the case as a childish trick).

It was rumored a few days later that it was mistaken identity, which had started the whole incident. It was not R' Chaim Voysekhovitser's daughter who was seen in the crowd, but a pure born Catholic girl. Our sages said:" Don't panic", "Act only when it is clear as the sun". It was not far from developing into a real disaster.

R' Chaim Voysekhovitser's daughter returned later to Judaism. He married her with a scholar but a poor Jewish boy, and had the pleasure of seeing his grandchildren grow up to be fine Jews.

R' Menachem Eizenberg lived in the same village. He was a pious Jew who had a house with a store and a tavern. His son, R' Shlomo who was R' Tzvi Rubin's son-in-law. He moved to the town and had a store in R' Tzvi's house.

Dzhurov

A few Russian immigrants lived in this village. They came with the righteous R' Yisrael from Rizin who fled Russia in 1840.

R' Yakov Alter leased a property and a whiskey distillery where he and his sons, who were fine Jews, worked.

R' Shmuel Alter was a pious Jew who had a house and a store where his wife, Rachel, worked while he sat and learned Torah. He and his wife Rachel died in Zefat in 1895. His sons R' Menachem, R' Yoseph and R' Tuvia were educated in Torah, the fear of God and became important merchants. R' Shmuel's grandson, R' Moshe Alter, a scholar, emigrated to Berlin and later, during Hitler's rise in Germany he emigrated to Eretz Yisrael where he purchased a house on Sheinkin Street (in Tel-Aviv). R' Shmuel's son-in-law, R' Yakov Menachem Gaster, was a scholar who learned the mysteries of the Jewish Kabala, was a Visnica's Chasid. In his late years he moved to Kuty where he died.

R' Moshe Gaster a scholar, a wonderful mathematician, a bookkeeper and an accountant for the whiskey distillery and his father-in-law R' M.L. Shlumiuk's farm. He educated his sons in Torah and the fear of God. His son, R' Chaim Gaster was a great scholar who later moved to live with his father-in-law in Botshatsh. His son-in-law, R' Mordechai Halprin, owned land in Voruchta.

R' Naftali Weinberg, a scholar who leased land in the village.

Chalibitchin

R' Baruch Meltzer the Village Elder was a clerk for the owner of the Estate. His sons were educated in Torah. His son R' Yoseph Leib and his wife Sara Tila had a tavern in Turka. They gave to charities and were hospitable to guests.. They educated their sons in Torah and crafts. His daughter, Hela, married a Jewish Scholar who had a grocery store in the village.

R' Yakov Toy (nicknamed Tebrek) leased the village mill and fields for farming. Later he purchased and lived in a large house in Zablotow's market square. He was a land broker and very accepted by Avramovitch who owned three large estates. He was a very successful broker, became very rich, powerful and forceful. He demanded respect and through his cunning ways he was elected to City Council.

Tulukow

R' Elezer Shtadler and his sons R' Moshe and R' Yisrael leased the large estate from Agifsovitch. They were very successful, had many guests, gave a lot to charities, especially R' Yisrael's wife, Tova, the daughter of Aaron. R' Yeshaya Adlershtein and R' Sh. Toy took over the lease of the estate after the Shtadlers left. R' Yehuda Singer leased the large tavern. Had some land and was a land broker. R' Manle Hirsh Libs was a pious Jew who had a house in the village and dealt in wood for heating. Educated his son in Torah. His son Alter learned Gemara, Bible, and later became a grain dealer.

Trachi (Trojca)

Trachi was a large village belonging to Avramovitch and his sons.

R' Zalman Hibner from Kolomyja leased the large mill. R' David Meltzer was the manager. There were a few other Jews working in the mill and collecting wood for heating, and lived frugally.

R' Tzvi Aryeh Leviner was a clerk for Avramovitch most of his life. He and his wife, Tova, donated to charity and were hospitable (Tova lived to the ripe old age of over one hundred). They educated their sons in Torah. Shmayah was a grain dealer and had a store in Viena. Menachem was a clerk in a number of saw mills, the last one was in Otynya.

R' Yisrael Libber and his son Menachem were Kosov Chasidim and had some land. His widow, Tima, lives in Tel-Aviv, Israel with her daughter.

R' Yeshayahu Shfarber and his son-in-law R' Berel were honest men, Kosov's Chasidim. R' Menashe Shfarber from the village of Dardaus next to Trachi was an honest man who owned some land and was R' Yitzchak Tilinger's father-in-law.

Troschinich (Druzhinets)

R' Anchel Kalman who was a dear Jew and an enthusiastic and trusted Zionist lived here. The first Zionist pioneers trained in farming for their life in Eretz Yisrael on his estate and he was their mentor and spiritual father. His only daughter, Yehudit, emigrated to Eretz Yisrael where she eventually became a devout Communist. She now lives abroad.

Roznov

Roznov was a large village or a small town where about sixty Jewish families lived including a rabbi, a slaughterer, a public bath etc. Thursday was market day when merchants from the surrounding and from Zablotow displayed their produce, buying and selling thus providing income for the locals.

Rabbi Itchele (R' Yitzchak Meir) R' Mendele's grandson from Demycze. R' Yeshaya Rottfeld was the slaughterer. R' Efrayim R' Yerachmiel Bergman's son was a scholar, had a large house a store and a tavern. His grandsons live in Israel working in farming. The widow Shlima, R' Efrayim's sister owned a large house and many properties. She was a merchant. R' Yisrael Singer, a brother of R' Chaim Zimel, was a respected man, owned a large house, a hotel and Tavern He was busy with community work and educated his son and daughter in Torah and general education.

Rudniki

The whole village belonged to Maissi who was an Anti-Semite Polish senator who leased his properties to Jews only. The forests of strong birch and pines where used for wood and lumber. His large mill, the whiskey distilleries, the farm etc. were all leased to Jews who lived comfortably.

R' Shmuel Pesach was an honest man, a pious Jew who owned some land. Following his marriage he had a store at his father-in-law's house, but after his wife died he moved to Kolomyja and became a contractor for the Army. His brother David remained in Rudniki and participated with his father in his business.

R' Tzvi Herman leased a farm and a tavern with a store. His wife, Freida, the only sister of R' Yechiel Mechel Karsel, was a very capable and smart woman. She took care of their business. Their only daughter, Babche, married R' Yakov Toy, son of Chaim from Zablotow who inherited his father's house in the market square. They had a successful hotel, restaurant and a tavern. They and their children perished during the Holocaust.

The Town Where I was born

By Meir Heinish

Zablotow, the town where I was born and which was the background of my youth and adolescence, looked at that time like all the other Jewish towns and Shtetls in eastern Galicia. Although the main trains line from Lwow to Chernovtsy passed through our town, it was still like a hole in the middle of no-where as far as its cultural level and people's knowledge about world affairs was concerned. Not much was absorbed by them from all the spiritual aspirations, which came from Kolomyja in the west or from Chernovtsy the Capital City of Bukovina, definitely not enough to nudge my sleeping town out of its frozen cultural state. Except for a very few who were the Jewish Professional Intellectuals (The Notary, Doctor, Pharmacist etc.) who actually had no real interaction with the Jewish community and a few other educated families who had no affect on the town. The majority of the Jewish community did not acquire general knowledge and education. The Jewish Tradition was deeply rooted in every aspect, and each activity was in accordance with the proper Jewish way of life, almost with out exception. Since worship was more important than Torah studies, the Chasidic Movement and its variations took a strong hold in town and most Jews congregated under various dynasties of Rabbis. On the other hand there were very few of the town's own learned, but they did not have a great number of followers and none had spread his wisdom by writing a book of Midrash (homiletic interpretation) or Scholastic nature. From these I only remember three. R' Alter Parless, who was a member of Beit-Din (Jewish Court) and was highly thought of by R' Meir Ish-Shalom, lecturer at the Biet-Hamidrash (Jewish school) in Vienna, whom he met while in Vienna for his wife's medical treatment. The second was L. A. who was very smart, sharp and knowledgeable in Talmud, but "the delicate wine was in an ugly bottle". He was often found drunk and lying in gutters. The third was R' David Hersh who was my Rabbi for a short time. Although clever and knowledgeable in Talmud, bright and quick students would not stay with him since his methods were slow and repetitive. I used to cynically categorize his method as "Regurgitating but without split hooves", not advancing a mile. (Hooves and a mile are homonym in Hebrew).

Unlike other Jewish communities, there was no Chief City Rabbi in Zablotow, but rather two Rabanim, Yakov and his brother Mendel Hager, sons of R' David Hager (son of R' Mendel from Kosov). Each one saw himself as the heir of his father's position and each established his place in this small town causing a split, by establishing his own synagogue and having his own followers (one in center of town, the other in the suburb of Demycze). The Chasidim who belonged to the Kosov Dynasty followed mainly the first, while the Viznica Chasidim followed his brother. Only R' Mendel From Demycze was still alive when I was young and his position was inherited by his grandson Avraham, from his daughter Gitele, while R' Menachem Mendel, the only son of Yakov was already in the Rabbi's chair in Zablotow. The same hatred, which existed between the brothers, stemming from competition in making a living, from the will to control the community, and the wish to have the power to appoint the slaughterers, also prevailed with their descendents. Appointing the slaughterers was a source of major problems, but they circumvented the other disagreements by having separate committees for each part of the community. I remember a major uproar when a third Rabbi was appointed from among the Kosov community, which caused the community to split in the middle, and it deteriorated to a point where people caused physical harm to one another, committing sins and desecrating the Name of God. I was to blame too, as I was not only a passive witness but participated in the preparation, printing and distribution of nasty announcements against the Rabbi, calling for his boycott and excommunication. This dispute lasted for a long time and died out slowly after a special Rabbinical court was appointed (made up of R' Feivel Shrier from Borodshin and R' Yacov from Kolomyja).

A Jewish community cannot survive solely with slaughterers and Rabbis who only prayed and had their father's credit, it needs a righteous teacher and a capable judge. Thus each Rabbi had a Jewish Dayan in his synagogue for the purpose of providing their constituents answers to what is right or wrong and judging in monetary disputes. They, like their leaders, hated each other and did not venture out of their respective areas. Each part of the community was careful to ask for a decision solely from its respective leader. (I remember being sent a few times by my grandfather from our house in the suburb to the Rabbi in town and how careful I was not to ask a question from the other Rabbi even though he lived very close to us).

There wasn't a single educational or cultural institute, or an elementary school, or a technical school for Jewish children in our community. In later years when Baron Hirsh sponsored an Elementary Jewish School in town, the citizens did not approve of it, and mainly poor families sent their children there, for the free food and clothing which were handed out there. Not a single social institution or a single charity organization existed in town. The few Zionists who lived in town and followed the "Love of Zion" organization of Tarnow (established by Dr. Zaltz), were not actually accepted into the organization, but only participated in collecting donations for the settlement of Eretz-Yisrael during prayers of The Day of Atonement. I recall how fascinated I was by that miserable lonely collection plate with a "For Eretz-Yisrael Settlement" note in it, placed together with a few other plates on a table at the entrance to the synagogue, being ignored by everyone, and no pennies being placed in it. Once, when I noticed the attendants nudging this plate and moving it away from all the others, I had the courage to put it back with all the others, thus becoming its self-proclaimed 'guardian'. With penetrating eyes I looked into the hands of the people, and in my heart I prayed that they would donate a few pennies and would not insult it. In later years when the Zionist movement seeped into all corners of the world, our town too, had a Zionist Group approximately at the same time when a philanthropic group was also formed (called 'Friends for Refuge"), but both did not last long. Apparently, our town was not yet worthy.

This environment did not have a positive effect on the young generation of our town, on its education and on its cultural development. Most of the youth growing up in town were uneducated, uncivilized and later even without Torah. Despite the strict adherence to the Jewish traditional way of life, modern spirits influenced the youth, opened their eyes and diminished their will to continue studying arcane useless subjects. Students in Beit Hamidrash disappeared one by one and moved on to study general studies eventually becoming 'educated' and did not further pursue Torah studies. Nevertheless, their self-acquired education was mostly superficial since it was informal and was not acquired in a methodical organized fashion, and not by a proper teaching staff. Usually, their education consisted of Hebrew books, then progressed to classic German. The Polish language was not required since the surrounding population was Ruthenian - they absorbed very little of what they read, thus not acquiring a valued education, but rather paved the way to cheap literature and the occasional German newspapers.

This situation did not usually cause a change in their way of life. Being 'educated' they still preferred the lazy way of life being supported by their parents until they established their own family, continuing their laziness while now being supported by their in-laws. Only very few dared to leave town and wander into the world, doing it more out of necessity due to personal or family conditions, and not by choice. Most of them prospered in time in their new locations, whether it was Germany or across the ocean, and then forgot their origin. Very few succeeded in becoming community leaders in their own right. My good friend Mr. Yissachar Toy, whose economical success in New York and his vast business activities did not distract him as he kept his Jewish spark and his Zionist past. He became a distinguished figure in the management of "The Galician Pravand" and in the Zionist Organization of New York. He also supported many Hebrew writers and kept in-touch with Eretz-Yisrael where he visited a few times. He did not forget his hometown either, and donated from his fortune to its institutions, especially to the Jewish School. In contrast to Mr. Toy, we note Mr. Yehuda Tilinger also from Zablotow, who caused a great shame to his people and origin. Being a descendant of a well-respected family of Religious Chasidim and a talented scholar, he nevertheless deserted his wife and daughter in Bukovina and immigrated to Germany where he attended university and a rabbinical seminar. He received a Doctorate in Philosophy and served for a short time as a Rabbi and a religious teacher in the community of Nordan in Berlin. Suddenly, an evil spirit took hold of him, he turned away from Judaism and even publicly scorned the Jewish faith and its Torah. I remember the storm created when the news about his behavior reached our town. I read the letter he sent from Germany to his family in Zablotow, in which he pretended to be persecuted by his personal rivals (in particular he mentioned Dr. Maibaum from Berlin). After this incident he disappeared and was forgotten, until he resurfaced later as a Rabbi of a small congregation in a small town in the United States. The American Jewish press uncovered his past, publicly shamed him, and the Rabbinical Council publicly tried him.

The social fabric of the Jewish population in Zablotow did not differ from most other towns of Galicia, especially in Pokutia District. The majority of the population were pragmatic merchants and dealers, store owners or had stands in the City Market, wheelers & dealers of whatever they could get their hands on, roaming the streets aimlessly, looking for an occasional windfall. There were only a few mechanics and artisans who worked all day and into the night in order to support their families. There were a handful of wealthy property owners and rich individuals who dealt in currencies, and interest-baring loans. Then there were the vast number of activists related to religion: Rabanim, Dayan, Kashrut Inspectors, Cantors, Teachers, Gabaim, Scribes, and simple Jews, bums and the poor, all of them were a constant burden on the community.

The community could not support itself, but luckily the town was situated in the midst of many Ukrainian villages. God granted the Jews with the wisdom to declare every Tuesday a Market Day, when all the villagers flocked into town to buy or exchange merchandise. The days prior to Market Day were days of anxiety and preparations. Storeowners were busy restocking and filling their warehouses with items of the season. Some were smart enough to prepare stands and tables for their merchandise in the middle of the City Square. Grain dealers, chicken or cattle merchants ran around looking for "charity" for Market Day. All others who were "potential" dealers fought amongst themselves while eagerly waiting for the market, praying that God Almighty would not forget them and will provide them at least with a chicken for Shabbos, and maybe even with some profit.

The town transformed into a bustling city during Market Days, even if not always attracting the expected results, it still brought many villagers into town. They sold their produce and their cattle, and in exchange bought all they needed for their homes and fields, thus becoming the main source of income for this Jewish town.

Another source of income was the Tobacco factory, one of few which were built in Galicia by the owner of the Tobacco monopoly. The Jewish population did not directly enjoy any profit from the factory since no Jew was found among its many workers or managers. The Jewish population did not choose to refrain from working there, because despite their psychological religious inhibitions it is quite certain that at least few Jews would have been ready to work there, if not for the Polish Authority's strict refusal which stemmed from Anti-Semitism. But indirectly the Jews profited greatly from the factory especially during the first few years of operation, when the workers, mostly Ukrainian peasant, spent their earnings in town. The Jewish owners of restaurants and taverns enjoyed great incomes when the workers spent their earning on lunches. Storekeeper sold their merchandise to the workers who purchased clothing and other necessities, and craftsmen too, earned good incomes. This was especially true during the winter months when the tobacco growers flocked into town with their crops. It usually took a couple of days for them to complete their transactions and in the meantime they lodged in hotels or private homes, drank and dined, spent large sums of money purchasing goods and presents for their families, thus profiting the Jewish population.

This was a mixed blessing for Jews. During that period a new Ruthenian National Movement was established in Galicia which intended to rid itself or the Polish burden. The Poles were the rulers on behalf of the Austrian Government, they oppressed and humiliated the Ruthenians, who in-turn used the helpless Jews as scapegoats. The long existing hatred of the Jews by the Ukrainians blurred the clear vision of the leaders of the new movement and they considered the Jews to be the main cause of the poor economic and political state of the Ruthenian Nation. Their inciting propaganda was directed against the Jews but it did not last, since the Ruthenians were uneducated and scattered all around in isolated farms and villages. Modern means of communication did not yet exist, making it impossible to mobilize them against the Jews. The Tobacco factory was a perfect greenhouse for the new movement and its Anti-Semitic ideas. Like all other industry workers, they were easily convinced to accept the poisonous hatred against the Jews and spread it into their farms and villages. It is therefore not surprising to find that Zablotow was one of the first towns in Galicia where Ukrainian stores where set up to provide business competition with the Jews. It was in Zablotow where the Anti-Semitism theory was developed and flourished, and where Pogroms were carried out against the Jewish population in 1903, exactly when the large pogroms happened in Czarist Russia.

Zablotow's Pogroms of 1903

By Meir Henish

On Friday night, September 11 1903, The Zionists in Kolomyja received a Telegraph from Zablotow informing them a Pogrom broke out in town that day during the Halawsiki market. Without further ado two "Beitar" members were summoned to Zablotow and those remaining in Kolomyja armed themselves and got ready to go to Zablotow to protect the Jews over there. But things calmed down the next day and the two members returned to Kolomyja. I did not calm down; Zablotow was my birthplace, the town I had just left and where all my friends were. I immediately decided to go there, but waited till Sunday.

I am not sure whether it was a spur of the moment decision or was it my increasing political and practical sense influenced by recent events, but I remember being the first to understand the urgency of the situation. I convinced a few others and we organized a delegation to Zablotow to investigate in detail what had happened there and record the events while the memory was still fresh. Two other Zionists from Kolomyja joined me, one being a lawyer, and the three of us arrived on the scene as a formal delegation.

The news about the arrival of the delegation spread fast, and within an hour many of the witnesses gathered around, including some of the wounded, and we visited the homes of those who were more seriously wounded. It became immediately apparent, as we had originally suspected, that it was not a spur of the moment outburst of violence against the Jews, but rather it was a well planned and orchestrated instigation which started in the villages by political agents, stemming from the political and economic conditions. The anger of the mass of Ruthenian farmers who were organized into local radical nationalistic groups was directed mainly at the ruling Shlicht (Nobility) who oppressed and humiliated the Ruthenians.

The various local governing bodies who were themselves subordinates of the Shlicht, assisted the Shlicht in the oppression, using the Jews to carry it out. It served them twofold; Firstly, that the Poles were assured a greater majority over the Ruthenians, and secondly, the oppressed and deprived farmers directed all their anger and vengeance towards the Jews and not at the Poles or the ruling Shlicht. It was prepared under the slogan "Hit on the Liachs (Slur for Poles) and the Jews". It was not a surprise that the violence, which was at first directed against the Poles and the Jews, turned solely against the Jews, and was not squashed by the authorities that stood watching from the side. The organizers neglected the political and economical causes of the outbreak, but used the well known "Blood Accusation" yelling "The Jews had slaughtered a woman peasant and hid her". The farmers who came to the market hit and beat the Jews by the orders of the local government officer Skalski, and the storeowner Karschivaski, both native Poles. The Gendarmes, who were called in, took their time, and the Post Officer clerk did not rush to send telegrams calling for help.

Another unexpected thing became apparent to us. Some of the witnesses and the wounded themselves refused to reveal all they knew and refrained from lodging official complaints, whether from fear of retaliation or from the apprehension of monetary losses. It is hard to describe how depressing it was for us to see how, only one day after the Pogrom, the victims themselves wished to conceal and hide the facts. To our dismay we found ourselves, a delegation of outsiders, in the peculiar and very uncomfortable position of trying to assist those who did not wish to be helped at all, and instead of accepting the comfort offered them they were saying: Take your goodwill and spread it elsewhere. We were happy to find a few whom still had the personal courage to come forward, thus we were still able to gather enough written affidavits. It is important to mention that typically those were mainly the mechanics and artisans and the simple Jewish farmers, while the merchants, storekeepers and bartenders usually tended to hide and conceal the facts.

When I returned to Kolomyja with all the material I had collected, I had virtually no one to hand it over to and I realized that I had not concluded my mission but that it had just begun. According to my suggestion, a committee was established to handle the subject, comprising of Dr. Rosenhak as chairman and myself as Secretary. My first action was to publicize it in the local newspapers, and also in the country news, in-order to create public pressure on the authorities not to ignore it, as they had done in similar incidents, but to bring to justice those responsible. The essence of the events was provided to the press and I myself published the main facts in two articles in "Hatsfira" (issues 204 & 218 in 1903).

Another important task of the committee was to appoint a representative in the claims by the Jews who were affected. Union Company of Vienna summoned its Secretary, Mr. Zigmond Fleisher, to Zablotow immediately, and on his way back he passed through Kolomyja and, on his own, appointed the Lawyer Dr. Shor to be their representative in Kolomyja. The appointment did not sit well with Kolomyja's Jewish population, especially since he was the head of the local PPS (Polish Social Democratic Party), and distanced himself from

Jews and Judaism. Furthermore, just prior to his appointment, Dr. Shor blamed publicly the Zablotow's Jews themselves for causing the Pogroms by their attitude towards the local farmers. With the intervention of our committee his appointment was canceled by Union Company and handed over to Lawyer Dr. Tchipser, as suggested by our committee.

After five months of great effort by the committee, the instigators of and participants in the Pogroms were brought to court in Kolomyja (in 25.02.1904). The prosecution representing the Jews was properly prepared, and the Press both within Poland and outside, showed interest and covered the progress of the case. The other side did not sit idle either; a group of lawyers headed by the head of the Ruthenian "Sitch" movement, Dr. Trilovski of Kolomyja, handled the defense. Experts to lie and deceit methodically trained the defendants and their witnesses. The Jews were greatly disappointed by the outcome of the trial, which handed the rioters and criminals' only light sentences, while the real instigators were completely acquitted. Nevertheless, it is safe to assume that the efforts exerted by the Jews in connection with the trial and the publicity it had received, were not all in vain. No further Pogroms were carried out in Galicia - even those already planned - in this wild and cruel fashion, probably because they realized that somebody is watching them and the Jews knew how to defend themselves, too.

At the conclusion of my involvement with the Pogrom of Zablotow, I published in "Welt" (issues 10 and 12 in 1905) a summary of the trial and its consequences.

Zablotow between the Two Wars

By Avraham Karsel

Prior to starting to note my memories of the Zionist movement in Zablotow, I would mention the names of a few of my best friends like. Selig Gross - My mentor in Zionism, Netanel Goldner-Freidman, Yosef Koren, Yehoshua Gross, Leib Rubin, Moshe Rubin, etc. who worked with me and dedicated most of their wealth and strength to the Zionist Movement of Zablotow during the years between the two wars.

Few Zionist were there in Zablotow to start with. I remember the night of our great fire of 1911, when most of the houses downtown were gutted - from Zalman Donest's house to the house of Hirsch Leib Nates Zeinreich (our house too, as well as the Rabbi's house, were completely burnt then). That night, 20 of Tamuz, I walked home late at night from the memorial to Hertzl. I still remember the speech: During the month of Tamuz Dr. Hertzl died, and Tamuz means "End of Strength" in Hebrew. But the Zionism as a thriving movement, active in public life started to be active only after the First WW. The first action was the "Nationalrat" at the time of the Ukraine's, when we 'conquered' the community and removed the Gabaim from office. I also remember the first meeting at the City's Beth Midrash (Studet Beth Midrash), with Chaim Toy (Yukiles) getting out shamefully, when he realized whom he had to hand over the rains of the Community to. Rabbi Itsche Tilinger told me right then: Avreme'le, you know that a fresh garlic has strong taste, but it's better to use old one for cooking meat". By that he wished to eliminate the young generation, that was not ready to manage public matters. But the honeymoon of the Zionist rule did not last long. The internal quarrels between the pro Shtudeter Rabbi and the Demycze (Tumizher) rabbi pushed us, the Zionists, outwards and maybe it was for the better, since this way we were free to devote all our energy to pure Zionist matters.

Our town was at the bottom of the pole. The economic situation during these first years after the war was bad, and it dragged the cultural state with it. We hardly managed to open a Jewish school and it took inhuman efforts to balance its budget. Once we were helped by MTT Association of Lewow, and another time a by an American passerby who originated from Zablotow, and donated a certain amount to the school. On the other hand, the Youth movement thrived and we were encouraged by it for our public and cultural activities. It is worth mentioning here the Chanukah and Purim festivals, the garden festivities at Yacov Weich's estate in Tulukov, where the Hachshara Group had stayed and in our

Community Hall. The garden festival covered most of the cost of running our group. It also worth mentioning the great library with few languages: German, Hebrew, Polish and Yiddish that helped significantly raising the cultural level of the youth and the public.

Those days - being days of distress and of shortage - when we suddenly stood at a point where we had to close the Jewish school, which had already establish itself, appeared the lovely personality of Reb Yisachar Toy from USA. He arrived then from Israel and came to visit Zablotow full of desire to help needy brethren. At the Zionist Committee we explained to him the situation the school and the city were in. We wished to have the poor kids enrolled in the school, and not only the rich ones, since the poor were the ones who participated in the Zionist youth movement and they were those who immigrated to Israel.

Mr. Yisachar Toy, the good hearted, generous and Zionist activist, promised us not only a hefty monitory assistance, but also took it upon himself, once he returns home, to get the rest of the Jews who originated from Zablotow, to help our school. And so it was. A short time afterwards we received a message that a Committee for the Jewish School in Zablotow was established in the USA. They have collected monies and wanted to purchase a house for our school, which enabled the purchase of the "National House". At the same time that house caused us troubles, since it brought with it quarrels and fights which took of our time and caused a waste of effort and neglect of the main Zionist activity. This is also one of the reasons that during those years the immigration to Israel had dwindled, in contrast to other nearby cities. Nevertheless, we can not diminish the dedicated work that was done over the years by the Zionists in Zablotow. The writer of these lines, one of only few survivors, will not forget the dedication with which the dear friends performed the Zionist tasks in Zablotow.

It is worth mentioning in this opportunity our friend, the dear Zionist, living with us here in Israel, being R' Avraham Gross, who immigrated with his family. Not only one house he sold to get to Israel (before the first WW) and finally made it to Israel in 1922 almost empty-handed (he hardly gathered enough to sell for the expense of the trip). Who will forget his loud thunderous Zionist speeches at the Great Synagogue during the confirmation of the British Mandate - a short time before he immigrated to Israel - "This is the day God has created, we shall rejoice it and be happy". He was the one who established before the war the Yeshiva of Zablotow at the house of R' Elyahu Bergman in Demycze. With his hot temper and warm enthusiasm for every thing cultural and of National essence, he pulled into it the Rabbi of Demycze. Even though modern spirits came out of the Yeshiva, the best people of the town gave it a helping hand. I will mention two interesting incidents from the Yeshiva:

When the Rabbi of Kopitschinsz came to visit Zablotow, we were invited to the Yeshiva. I was in First Grade. The Rabbi entered the classroom and placed me on his lap, I uttered a page of Gemara (Baba Metziah) by heart while R' Avraham Gross stood at the side greening joyously.

During the winter of 1907 and 1908.

Our R' Avraham Gross acting as a manager and a guide, or better as the owner of the Yeshiva, had a special room, where each day he locked himself there and no one knew what he was doing. We were very curious to find out the secret. We did not spear any mischief to find it out, but to no avail. Suddenly, one Thursday night, with Shabbos spirit already upon us, when the studies are a bit lax and we study Torah reading or "Or Chaim", there he was. R' Avraham Gross ceased the lectures and asked all to enter his "secret" room. We stood elated and surprised at the entrance to see the Desert Tabernacle complete from the Tenons (foundations), Curtains, Boards, till the Cover, Table etc. etc. He went over it with us, explaining each and every detail, and it is very hard to explain how hard he worked at it. It goes without saying that all the Jews of our town flocked over to the Yeshiva to witness the wonder.

The Yeshiva did not last long and closed after two years, since his obstacle was his Zionism, which he mentioned on all occasions and opportunity. Even his dances at the Rabbi's house did not stand for him with the people of our city.

I should also mention the house of R' David Hersch Shochet (Gross) including his sons and daughters. That House, with capital letters, had seen everything; the finest Zablotow's Zionism in its inception, the various Youth movements, Zionist singing crowds on Saturday nights, who can not remember these? The first Jewish school, the library, Zionist Yeshivas, Youth meetings and numerous preparations for parties and Zionist events. It all took place in this worm and important house. Mr. Zelig Gross personality shined through, he was the main organizer of the Zablotow's Zionism. We were all his Zionist followers. He was the man behind the establishment of the library in 1918, the backbone of the "Nationalrat" at the time of the Ukraine's. I still remember his first boisterous speech at the founding of the "Nationalrat" with his powerful talk persuading the crowd to join. Throughout his years, till the Nazis murdered him, he sacrificed his complete being and time for Zionism and for the Zablotow community. He was studying in Vienna before the first WW when the Zionist movement engulfed him, he interrupted his studies, and joined the movement with his worm passion. His influence on his surrounding, the youth, the whole town was indescribable, despite his usual poor health state.

I will add few of my best friends, who participated in the Zionist Movement in our town:

Mr. Netanel Goldner (nick named Sani). It was at a very early age when we sat together in Bais Hamidrash of the Stodeter Rabbi learning Gemara, that we became very close friends, loving each other like David and Yonathan. When he returned home as an amputee from the First WW his house was transformed to be the permanent Yeshiva. Not a single day passed in which we did not seat until the late hours of the night, despite me being occupied with my business and many jobs I had. We became known, as Siamese twins, whom one can not survive without the other, like a body with out the soul, or vice versa. It was worth getting dirty in this dear man's dust. He possessed a tremendously vast knowledge both in our ancient literature and in the common literature. He also possessed a surprising and phenomenal memory. He was honest but did not restrain himself from voicing his opinion about anyone and directly to him. He was admired by all; the conscience of our movement. If it became known that Sani promoted or approved an idea, it was instantly agreed by all. This good friend possessed abundance of energy and courage. He was the promoter and the life behind each and every Zionist activity in our town, its institutions, including the Youth movements, library, Jewish school, and also political activities, elections for the Saim, for the community etc. it was he who paved the way. It was all done in Sani's room and I am proud to have been there with him. He was taken to Kolomyja's Ghetto at the conclusion of the cruel destruction of the Zablotow's Jewry, but even there found a way to be active. He carefully wrote down and noted the entire cruelty-taking place in Zablotow, but to our dismay, he too was killed with all the rest. May he rest in peace.

Mr. Yosef Koren. "Silk Yeshiva Student" was his nickname, at the time he was "bought" by one of the riche men, Mr. Zalman Freminger, and wed his eldest daughter, since he was loaded with Torah and general knowledge. Arriving in Zablotow he dedicated his time to Zionism and did not listen to curses and abuses from his close family. He neglected his own business, and supported our cause from his own resources, especially the school and the "National House". Large sums were required to purchase the house, and he loaned money to others so they can pay their dues; these funds were never returned to him. As the eternal "president" of the Zionism in our town he suffered greatly from the quarrels and internal fights. With his soft personality, good heart and irony he managed to find the right words to bring people back together. He always knew to find the center road and show us the avenue to success. It was him who persuaded Zablotow's immigrants in USA to carry the burden of purchasing the house and the institute, so great was his influence and persuasive power on them, especially on R' Yisachr Toy A"H. May he rest in peace.

Days Gone By

By Esther Karsel

Memories of my youth in my hometown are forever etched in my heart. I will recall some of them in the following pages as a tribute to "Days Gone By".

The first event I remember was when the first three street lampposts were installed in the main street of Zablotow. We, a group of happy joyous kids, stood there watching those poles as if they were a miracle. Our parents had to drag us away. Another "miracle" was electricity, which was installed for the first time in town in the new fabric factory. Group after group - grownups included - walked to see the sight of electric lights.

A Jewish school existed in Zablotow before the First World War where we studied in the afternoons, while the morning were spent in the official Polish School.

I was a toddler when a great fire roared through our town and destroyed most of the houses. I remember a strange thing. A short time before the fire broke out, I heard a strange noise emanating from my parent's room. I found the crib overturned and my younger brother lying on the floor. My father commented that it must be a sign of an approaching disaster, which soon came true.

Which child does not remember the First World War?

Loud trumpets called for mobilization and all the men rushed to the train station; it was on the ninth day of the month of Av 1914. A Typhus outbreak followed, creating havoc in town with every family suffering losses. The town was in quarantine and people were not allowed to hold funerals for their dead. Our dear father died then too, and only with great tricks did my brother manage to sneak away from the authorities and bury my father.

Zablotow was situated in the battle zone with hard battles being fought around it. It changed hands a few times causing great destruction, and many residents left town. They left their belonging in the hands of the "reliable" Ukrainians and wandered through the Karpathian Mountains to flee the battlefields. Our family wandered for days on end and my mother had to carry her young children alone until we came to a charming Check village, where we spent the rest of the war.

We returned home when Zablotow was freed, only to find it completely destroyed and devastated. In every house the doors, windows, floors etc. were torn out, but the returning residents embarked on rebuilding the town, and in a very short time it was restored and life return to its previous routine.

Figure 5. The First Pioneer Group from Zablotow in Eretz-Yisrael. Sitting, right to left: Yehudit Kalman, Ester Karsel. Standing, right to left: Bony (Avraham) Toy, Shchora Rosenboim, Elchanan Bloishtein.

Figure 6. Ha Shomer Ha Tzair Movement of Zablotow

The first years after the war were a new era in Zablotow. The young
men in town joined the Zionist movement and transformed the city into a
busy bustling place with many active Zionist Youth Movements, where
we trained for life in Eretz-Yisrael. We learned Hebrew, Jewish History,
the development of Zionism, fundamentals of Zionist labor, and all of us
were eager to leave Zablotow and immigrate to the Land of Our
Forefathers. We studied diligently the works of Gretz, Moshe Hess and
Martin Buber trying to penetrate and understand problems, which were
at first, far removed from us. We will always remember the trips to
Humow where we tried to sort things out as much as possible,
expressing naively our feelings with Israeli Songs. This is where the
decision to immigrate to Eretz-Yisrael and fulfill all these new ideas took
place.

When the time came to carry out that decision, one by one avoided it
citing all kind of excuses - Parents refusal, incompatibility with life in
Eretz-Yisrael and so on. How many tears did my mother shed trying to
prevent me from going, but I persisted. The blessed day finally arrived. It
was a cold winter day (December 1929), the sled whisked on the slippery
ice towards the train station. I turned to look at my house and town for
the last time, knowing that I will never return to see them again.

And I did not.

In the fields of the Galilee, the open-spaces of the Yisrael-Valley, the Swamps of Cabra, while paving roads in Judea and Samaryia, I remembered you my town. You had a lot of character; People and events, which forever will stir fond memories and sounds from your every corner.

Youth Movements

By Ms. Rachel Karsel

The seed of the pioneering Zionism planted in Zablotow during the days following the First World War gave shining fruit. The best of the youth were swept by the swift currents of Zionism, and fairly fast found a wide range for fruitful action in various areas which provided a sound basis for strengthening Zionism in town and its establishment in the hearts. The school and the library planted in each young boy and girl's heart the treasured revival. With a childish amazement I was faced with the charm of that period and got hooked. The affliction of youth fighting his parents, who are tuned to the order of a new generation, bothered me with so many questions: Why was the house disturbed? Why couldn't they continue in the old paved road? What caused them to stray from their parents' way? Why did they wish to form their own "groups"? How new and stimulating was the word "group" which then meant - lonely nights, sitting long hours in UN-heated rooms. How good it felt to be with your own age far from an atmosphere hostile to their feelings. During cold mornings the older ones left the bustling town, wandered to the mountains and forests, but felt stimulated and free. Those trips were filled with strong arguments and it was as if they were carried out in-order to flush out and express the last thought buried deep in the heart, and transfers it to others. A tiny, sweet drop of Clear Mountain air and the smell of the forest and flowers mixed in with their warm passionate temperament. The youth seized those experiences with passionate love and transformed them into rituals to which they sacrificed all that was dear and important.

The youth thus dedicated his life to Zionism in town and in the vicinity. Zionism broadened his horizon and gave him a different culture. It was a resurrection of both the body and the spirit. Youth of worthy ancestry became artisans and at once cut off the long tradition stating they didn't wish to be associated with it.

The town of Zablotow was a charming town, most of its people being merchants, surviving mainly on commerce with farmers from the vicinity. Many Gentiles came daily to town to do their commerce, but especially on Tuesdays, being the regular Market days. The town was bustling, every one who could was busy selling merchandise he was not dealing with during the rest of the week. The land situated between the small river and the Pruth River - where the cattle sales were held - was very noisy by the hand clapping of the various merchants. There were plenty of those selling baked goods and questionable quality colored drinks, but the farmers attacked it as if they were the best delicacies. Merchants from the vicinity (especially from Sn'yatin) drove into town with their wagons filled with merchandise. At nightfall when they returned with their owners sitting or lying on the empty boxes, young children roamed the empty area searching the mud for colored beads, which they strung into tradable items like their forefathers.

Sitting at home once, stringing my beads into a purse, I witnessed reading the Yizkor book for those of the Second Immigration wave (to Eretz-Yisrael) who perished on guard duty or at work. The impression this book had on me is unimaginable. It was partially in Yiddish and partly in Polish, and it formulated the realization methods youth followed those days. Reading the book took place in the first pioneer "group" in town (its members were: Bonio Toy, Bozio Lagshtein, Yehudit Kalman, Chana Greif, Batya Bernshtein and Esther Karsel). It was the tenth day in the month of Tevet, I wished to distract myself from the pain of the fast. After completing a row of green beads I felt it left a deep impression - this was a typical phrase heard in our group's discussions held in our home during the long winter nights. I was unintentionally charmed by some of the revelations made in this group, testifying how much they were accepted by the youth. That is how the pioneering idea grasped the youth and directed them towards a stubborn new way.

The core of the movement who managed to fulfill their ideas sent shock waves. A pioneer movement with many splinter groups sprang up in town, reaching its peak with "The Young Guard" (Hashomer Hatza'ir) movement during the years 1926 to 1931. During breaks in the Polish school we organized groups of children, visited homes in the poorer sections of town and took the kids to games which were mainly aimed at providing them with a collective experience. During Shabbos we gathered them for general discussions. The large number of kids who joined, since no other Zionist movement managed to attract them astonished us. We entered the homes of the artisans who were till then under the influence of the "Brotherstavo" (a local organization headed by Moshe Dunest with the declared object of spreading the Socialist Culture, but actually was busy defaming Zionism) . From these neighborhood we organized a group called "Workers" (Po'alim) where we combined Social ideas with Zionism into a single entity as we understood it and we prepared our trainees/friends to the life of work and communes in Yisrael. It was not easy, we used science, Biology, sociology and psychology to widen their horizon since they did not have formal school education, and they had been working all their young lives.

Just as the youth movement flourished for a few years and was a focal point for the entire active, Zionist movement, so it deteriorated after a few years. It was caused by many reasons but mainly due to the fact that no emigration was allowed and only a few managed to get through (to Eretz Yisrael). All the others, who did not possess the burning fire of rebellion against tradition their forefather's and customs of past generations in their hearts, stayed in town. But no doubt that belonging to the movement has left plenty of values even in the hearts of those dissidents, that lasted forever, and which manifested; a watchful and observant look at what was happening, an honest criticism, desire for simplicity, love of work and cultural awareness.

The peak of pioneer achievement was the establishment of the Hachshara in Tulukov next to Zablotow, where young boys and girls from Zablotow and the vicinity spent the entire day working in the fields and managing the farm itself. Nights were dedicated to cultural activities and in wondering about the first steps that would be required in order to fulfill their dream. Distant Tulukov became very close for a group of young girls, not yet ready for Hachshara. They went daily to Tulukov, short of breath, to witness in awe how the dream was shaping into reality. To hear first hand the experiences of the creator of all that, Bonio Toy, who had his hands in every Zionist pioneering activity in town for 15 years till his bitter demise (He choked to death in a box train-car). Zablotowers considered the Tulukov Project as a wonder and a crime. Many complained about the non-kosher food and strange behavior of the girls (a terrible combination). Whenever a pioneer form Tulukov came to town, people gazed at him with scorn, contempt and ridicule. A tall mountain stood between residents of the town and people from the Hachshara with a small chance of finding fathers with an understanding heart.

There were two places where youth gathered for organized Zionist activities. One was the bridge over the Pruth River and the meadow on both sides, which was the cradle of all activities. The meadow and the river with its permanent soft sound were silent witnesses to the formation of projects welcomed by many. Shabbos walks along the river inspired some glory into the hardships of everyday life. The second was the "Nationalhouse" which was the Zionist house purchased by our emigrants from Zablotow in the United States. The Zionist Movement settled in this house thus getting a permanent residency in town. Now they could demand more fiercely and with honor that people should listen and respond to what they had to offer.

Memory of dear characters who laid the foundations for Jewish-Zionist thought in town, now resurface. They belong to the senior generation who had that special rebellious ability, they neglected their own work and dedicated themselves to hard and dark, daily Zionist work. The first and foremost was Zelig Gross, who possessed the Zionist fire, and his thunderous rebellion against the generation's complacency erupted like a volcano, and his charming touch influenced many to join

Zionism. He was one of the only ones whose fiery Zionism did not extinguish in his heart and made him non-partisan. How sad it is that he did not manage to emigrate and share his abundant talent with our country.

Long is the list of the many dear people dedicated to Zionist activity in Zablotow but this platform is too short. My city is now destroyed, no monument can revive the glory hidden in its streets and allies saturated with Jewish life.

The Destruction of our Community

(As told by the survivors Tzvi Eizenkraft and Tzvi Freid)

The beginning of the end of our community was in September of 1939 when the Russian Army entered Zablotow. The whole population, with out an exception, welcomed the Russians with joyous cries and with festive welcoming ceremony by Mr. Moshe Donest (son of Mr. Zalman Donest) who soon after became the City Administrator. However, the joy was short lived. A majority of the citizens were evacuated from their homes, with the just emptied apartments handed over to Russian businesses and their workers. The rich were dispossessed of their belongings and deported to Russia - among them Mr. Leib Waller, deputy Mayor, a good hearted Jew with an open hand, who assisted many in their moments of need. All commerce in the city was halted and most merchants lost their employment. The city became a work camp. Workers breathed easily, but our Jewish brethren who did not experienced physical labor before, had to exert enormous efforts to convert to hard labor, however they were unsuccessful and hardly made ends meet.

The Zionist leaders in town, Mr. Josef Koren, Mr. Zelig Gross, Dr. Nusenblat, Mr. Lieb Rubin, Mr. Moshe Toy, Mr. Mendel Toy and alike, obtained Passports marking them as dangerous to Russia.

This situation remained static until the outbreak of the Russian-German war in 1941. The Russian Army left town in a hurry at the onslaught of the German invasion. The German Occupation Army with its Hungarian followers and allies entered the District of Kolomyja including our town. The Swastika flying at high mast together with the decrees that were already in place, were signals` to the bad times ahead and the Jews were trembling. The Hungarian Commander was not the worst, so Reb Avram Hagger, the Rabbi of Demycze (Tumizh) was able to establish a 'foot hold', which he used on many occasions for the benefit of the Community and individuals. However most of the troubles originated from the civil administrations, which were at the hands of the Ukraine's, who were the previous hooligans and murderers. They tortured the Jews and forced them into hard labor and used all possible means to starve the Jews including by preventing the local farmers from selling their produce to the Jews.

Starvation started affecting the Jews who at the same time were overburdens by hard labor. However, they comforted themselves saying their situation was still better then those who were under the control of the Real Murderers, the German Nazis.

This comfort was false too, since in August 1941 the German Nazis took over the area. Under the Hungarian occupation the Jews were subjected to theft and physical torture, now the Gestapo hinted immediately upon their arrival, that they will not stop at that, but rather wished to exterminate all the Jews including Christians of Jewish origin and converts. As a special sign to recognize all Jews, a shameful mark was established; made of yellow cloth marked with a Star of David. Every Jew was forced to wear this mark and those who refused were shot (few who did refused were actually shot).

Among the first decrees were the forbiddance of listening to radios, use of telephones, riding trains, and visiting public facilities such as: hospitals, bath-houses, coffee- shops, theatres, movie houses etc. A three member Jewish Council, "The Yudenrat" was established, they were: Mr. Neta Felix (Chairman), Mr. Elyahu Zinger and Mr. Efraim Fond. "The Council" was forced to ensure all decrees were fully complied with and they were personally responsible for it.

The first awful task of "The Council" was to establish various quotas for the murderers Nazis, for work force, for other purposes, and for their various needs. Their needs were growing and multiplying. Firstly they ordered for themselves all the gold and silver ware, furs, produce, cattle, and food items - and every thing under the threat of death. It was a heartbreaking sight to watch poor families bringing their only horse, or cow or goat to the location requested. They separated from the animals as if they were their best friend who were dying. But still they were unable to foresee that mush harder sacrifices are in future for them, and they are about to sacrifice their fathers, mothers, children - and all those whose life had no "purpose" for the murderers.

The Nazis did not have much satisfaction from this "Jewish Council" since they were unable to fulfil exactly their demands. Together with the District Jewish Council of Kolomyja, this Council was replaced and the new members were Dr. Teicher, Dr. Radish, Mr. Hertzl Unger and Mr. Shlomo Tilinger (the clerks of the old Council remained). The Gestapo, with the assistance of the local Ukraine's, extorted all the Jewish property and flesh, and this life-without-life continued until December of 1941.

First 'Action'

During December of 1941 special Gestapo personnel arrived at Zablotow to carry out their murderous plan. At Homov Hills (on the way to Troitsa) they ordered to dig huge holes the purpose of which escaped the Jews, however it became known to the citizens and there was a lot of confusion and embarrassment. A flight out of town began to wherever, only to escape until better times. The city emptied from Jews and only handful were left. When the Gestapo got hold of the situation they spread rumors that the digs were for protection against air raids. This way the Jews were persuaded to return to the city and they returned to the trap set up by the Gestapo. The Gestapo still waited for the last ones to return, and meantime the Jews relaxed until the terrible day of Chanuca 5702, 22.12.1941.

At that day, at 7 O'clock in the morning, the Gestapo burst into town from Kolomyja and attacked our poor brethren. Again, with the assistance of the local Ukraine's, armed with knives and axes, they surrounded the city. From street to street, house to house, the rioting murderers took out all Jews men women and children, beat them ferociously, shattered their skulls, poked their eyes and lead this half dead crowd to their death, like a flock of sheep, to the city market next to Golda Bartler's house. Mendel Toy Alters' eyes were poked out for his wife heroic resistance who screamed at her murderers a furious shout: "Our blood will not rest, Hitler will suffer a final loss, and Germany will pay dearly for her crimes". Mr. Elyahu Zinger yelled loudly prior to his execution not to hand over any money but rather to shred it to pieces. His last words were "Take revenge for our blood". Mothers' cry over their children froze the blood as they were killed together with the innocents.

The evil murderers urged the huge marching crowd on its death march towards Homov Hill with sticks and wild yells: "Les Les" (forward). At the head of this holy march stood Rabbi Avraham Hager, Rabbi of Demycze, and his wife and shouted:" Shma Yisrael, I lived with my brothers and I will perish with them".

When about a thousand arrived at the digs, they were placed in rows and lowered unto wood planks over the pits. Running on the planks they were shot, they fell, some dead some just wounded into the pits. Five strong Jews were ordered to straitened the corpses at the bottom of the pits, they were Mr. Yudel Bahn (son of Moshe Bahn), Nahum Zyler, son of Maytsch the carpenter and Tscupa Rubin. They were ordered to maximize the space and squeeze babies and small children in the corners. Those infants were not shot, in order to save on bullets, but had their heads smashed against the trees growing nearby and thrown into the pits. That was the fate of the infant just born to Alter Donuts daughter (wife of Harsh Hagar), to the baby of Ben-Zion Groundwork daughter and many more. The five men mentioned above got their rewards on the spot; one by one they were murdered too and their corpses were thrown in the pit. The ground that covered this holy grave of a thousand murdered Jews boiled from the blood that sprouted out, so they were forced to keep covering it with more earth. Mr. Ruben Toy, who worked with the Gestapo, managed to escape and made it eventually to our land. From here he immigrated overseas because of allegations that he collaborated with the murderers.

The 'Action' was completed by six O'clock in the evening. All the sick who were unable to get out, were shot in their beds. Thus there were about a hundred dead in the city itself, which were later brought to a Jewish Grave. There were those who elected to commit suicide rather then die at the hand of the murderers. Rabbi Yosel Eizenkraft (Koyne's) hanged himself, as did many others. Officially Mr. Netanel (Sani) Goldner was left alive as a disabled veteran of the previous war, and Dr. Nusenblat, wearer of war decorations. The nights following the 'Action' were used by the Ukraine's to ransack the empty Jewish homes and ruin them.

The following day, Zablotow's streets were riddled with awful cries, screams and shouts from each and every house. There was no house that did not suffer a loss. That same day at 10 O'clock before noon, the Gestapo came to the "Jewish Council" and demanded 10,000 gold coins for the cost of the bullets used to murder the Jews. They also demanded to gather all the belongings of the dead and hand it over to the Gestapo.

Second 'Action'

Cries of the events were still reverberating in the city and the next disaster was on the horizons. On the first day of Passover 5,702 (11.4.1942) The Ukraine's and the Germans ransacked the remaining Jews. They burst into homes with axes and hatchets and dragged out the living, ravaged every valuable property which were hidden and concealed; in most houses a hiding place was prepared for people together with hidden access. About 250 Jews were rounded up that day by the Gestapo, who were all sent to the crematoriums at Meydanek. At the beginning they were brought to the prison cells at the court house, where they were held for a few days without food or water till more Jews were brought in from the surrounding villages Il'intse, Popel'niki, Rudniki, Vashkovtsy, Kelikhov and more. Very few managed to redeem themselves at very exuberant cash amounts or valuable. All others were loaded onto boxcars still marked "garbage" and driven to Meydanek. Mr. Tzvi Freid, one of two witnesses who told this story, was freed from the gathering spot by his manager at 'Fast Technical Help' where he worked., together with others from the same office who held work permits. At that opportunity they were able to save some fifty more without papers and thus they were saved this time.

That same day, the second witness, Mr. Tzvi Eizenkraft, lost his sister, Kevina, and her 14 months old baby (according to the testimony of Izy the son of the hairdresser Yukev that jumped from the same boxcar and returned to Zablotow). She first choked her baby to death and then killed herself). The few Jews who survived in the City lived like the dead till the fifth of May 1942.

On that day a decree from Kolomyja arrived ordering all remaining Jews to leave Zablotow within three days and move to Kolomyja's Ghetto. After much endeavors it was prolonged by few days. At the agreed time the last Jews left Zablotow for the last time, except for about twenty who were left behind to gather and collect material. With the assistance of the Ukraine Militia, all the Jews were gathered and walked off to Kolomyja. Each was allowed to carry food and belongings totaling no more than 25 Kilos, and thus with their remaining ability they struggled to Kolomyja 20 Kilometers away carrying their personal loads. However, upon their arrival at Kolomyja they were robbed of their belongings and bitten up. Thus they arrived at the Ghetto empty handed, beaten and humiliated, with no food no clothing and no roof over their heads.

They lay in the streets and in ruins of the Synagogues. For each misdemeanor the Gestapo arrested them, and arrest meant death in Shiborovichi (a suburb of Kolomyja). Hunger was everywhere in the Ghetto and people lay in the street hunger stricken. The best of the youth wondered barefoot in the streets with swollen feet and faces, carrying pots begging to no avail for any food to revive themselves. Orphans roamed the streets lonely and deserted, torn clothes hanging from their swollen bellies, looking for leftover food in the garbage. People died daily and were buried in hiding for other to get their daily food ration.

Death struck more at those from the surroundings, since they came to the Ghetto empty handed. Mr. Netanel (Sani) Goldner kept record of the Zablotow's Jews who died, among them: Moshe Blei, Yosel Freminger and others. Few managed, for ransom, to obtain permits to return to Zablotow as workers, among them Doctors, Sani Goldner, Rabbi Damta (Rabbi of Shtudeter), Rabbi Chaim Hager, who worked head shaven with a casquette (cap) as a road worker on the road leading to Sniatin. Rabbi Mordeche'le Ashkenazi, the son in law of the Rabbi of Demycze, worked as a gravedigger at the cemetery. The witness, Tzvi Eizenkraft, was arrested by the Gestapo in Kolomyja for not properly greeting a German passerby in the street. After a few days he was released, only after his boss from the 'Tadet' work group had intervened. While in interrogations he witnessed the following: A 15-16 years old naked girl was brought in front of the head of the Gestapo. He interrogated her, the witness did not here what, and then the sadist opened a radio and a side door and let in a fierce Bulldog that ravaged the naked girl and bit her ferociously. As the girl's screams became louder and reached the sky, the sadist increased the level of the music emanating from the radio, till she fell down in a pool of her own blood. An order to take the 'garbage' out was heard immediately.

Again, about 250 Jews returned to Zablotow and were forced to work hard labor in public works. They exchanged their coats and last pants for a piece of bread from the local farmers who participated in the murder. Life continued that way till the last 'Action' on the seventh of September 1942.

Last 'Action'

Three days prior to the aforementioned day, it was ordered that the city be cleaned out (Yuden Rein). All the remaining Jews, including the "Jewish Council", were to walk to Sniatin to register. At two O'clock in the morning, about 250 people gathered to walk together to Sniatin in order to get there on time. Only about fifty people remained in the city, too old and weak, who hid in the city out of fear, and few who missed the time of the march. Among them: Dushka Zinger (Hiebsher, after she married) daughter of Riva Reisher and granddaughter of Otinya. It is worth mentioning here that until the last minute they did not at all suspected that they are going to be annihilated and destroyed. They still hoped deeply in their hearts that the scenes of the first "Actions" would not repeat, thus they walked freely to be registered.

Upon their arrival at Sniatin, the Gestapo like a chain with no possible escape route surrounded them. Only now they realized they were had. Then they were brought into a large room where the local Sniatin Jews and those from the surrounding villages, already waited. They were held there for four days with no food or water and in a suffocating environment. On the tenth of September they were made to run few Kilometers to the train station at Selishche and loaded unto box cars separated men and women. 150 people were squeezed into each car. On the way they were beaten, and especially tortured were the intelligent among them, Doctors, Lawyers, Pharmacists, etc. Dr. Nusenblat escaped so he will be shot and spare the sufferings. He got his wish. But the remainders, with a spark of hope in their hearts, gathered their diminishing strength and jumped out of the rolling car. Many were shot while jumping, only few managed to save their lives that way, among them Tzvi Freid, our witness, and Ruven Toy, mentioned above.

Those who remained in Zablotow were moved to Kolomyja Ghetto, which was exterminated in January of 1943. The murderers German with the active participation of their Ukraine helpers burned the Ghetto forcing all the Jews to come out of their hiding. Hundreds were burnt and those who fled the fire were shot and murdered in the streets. Only very few managed to escape to the forests, join the Partisans till the arrival of the Russian Soviet Army.

Micha Karsel

On the fourth day of Eyar 5708 (13.4.1948), one day before the declaration of our independence, in the fields of Kfar Hess, in a battle against our enemy - Yechiel Mechel (Micha) son of Avraham Karsel fell.

Figure 7. Micha Karsel & Zellig Gross

Figure 8. Kindergarten in Zablotow

Born in Zablotow in the month of Sivan 7686 (1926) he received his early education at the Jewish kindergarten in our town. His first days of school began when he emigrated with his parents to Eretz-Yisrael. In the melting pot where his parents had difficulty in their absorption in both work and agriculture, Micha was a gifted child who found school easy, had a smile that was a permanent fixture on his face and without which he could not be described. In Kfar Hess where his parents had settled, he was popular both at school and the youth movement. He had just graduated from school when the Nazi enemy approached our country, and at the age of 15½ he found himself joining the Army with his friends and serving in the British Army for more then four years. He matured during his service, wandering first in the desert and later in Italy, always reading a book keeping active. While in Italy he dedicated himself to the illegal emigration to Eretz-Yisrael, driving various cars day and night, he was very tired and was injured in a car accident just prior to his discharge.

He was discharged from the Army but not from active duty. Back in Kfar Hess, he was the head of the local Hagana group, and when fighting started following the UN declaration they protected their village which was near the Arab village of Tira, along the border of the country. This village was infested with murderers, which convinced him that it must be conquered in order to bring calm to the area of Tel-Mond.

In between various activities he was always reading and studying. His memory and understanding were incredible, his cultural awareness unimaginable. It was no wonder that he was very well versed in all aspects of Jewish literature and later in English literature as well, which he taught himself in his usual wonderfully carefree way. He tried to be the same as the "Tzabars" ridiculing Zionism, but deep inside he was different from them, making sure no one saw him during his "misconduct" absorbed in reading.

Sniper shots increased during the last month prior to the declaration, so he was at the head of the local group going out to battle and the first to fall. His blood touching his friends' blood and like some of them he does not reach eternal rest.

Zablotow of the Past

Mr. Avraham Keish

This is the Yiddish version of the Hebrew chapter.

The Destruction of Holy Zablotow Community

1. Description - Mr. Zvi Eizenkraft, Mr. Zvi Freid

(This is the Yiddish version of the Hebrew chapter)

2. Description - Mr. Zusha Toy

When the German army invaded East Galicia getting closer to our town of Zablotow every hour, the Jews started asking each other: "What will happen?" There were rumors that if we could cross the Russian border we could survive the war. However, all the roads were closed for the Jews and we had to take our chances and stay in our homes. Suddenly, on 17.9.1939, news arrived through the Russian radio that the Red Army was marching from the West and will settle in Eastern Poland. This caused some relief in the Jewish community. Anti-Semitism disappeared with the arrival of the Russian soldiers, Polish and Ukrainian Nazis converted immediately to be friends of the Jews since they realized how unsuccessful their ideology was. Each one of them became suddenly an honest man who lived comfortably with the Jews, and they tried to obtain good jobs at the Soviet Authorities declaring that they were Communists or at least they were sympathetic to Communism. Many Jews suffered materially and the morale was low due to the general Soviet system and their political ideology, but they all felt free, they worked and forgot about the danger, this was at the beginning of 1939. The Jews tried to integrate into the new situation, they became clerks, established Cooperatives in all trades and only a few stayed merchants, yearning for liquidation, in order to integrate themselves into the society of the new order. The honeymoon was short lived and in 1940 the Red Army started building large, strategic installations between Zablotow and Gewaztchich and erecting many fortifications along their west border, which signaled renewed danger for the Jews.

The great disaster did not take long to arrive. In the morning of June 22nd 1941 all the German radio stations announced that the Nazis had entered the Russian controlled area with the slogan "Death to the Jews". This terrible announcement did not have the expected result as the Jews could not believe that mass murders were in store for them, and they tried giving it other various explanations, each in accordance with his own understanding and beliefs.

The red Army retreated from our area in July with a few Jews who had the opportunity to join them. Most of the Jews fell into German hands and were killed by them. A few days after the Russian retreat, the Hungarian Occupying Army appeared which did not treat the Jews badly. They even voided some of the orders given by the murdering Ukrainians. Before the arrival of the Hungarian Army the Ukrainians killed the Jewish doctor Wolfram and his assistant Nisan Eizenkraft from Rudniki.

The Ukrainians raised their ugly heads when the Russians left the area and were ready to carry out Hitler's slogan "Death to the Jews". They were disappointed by the Hungarian soldiers and sent messages to the German command in Lemberg demanding the expulsion of the Hungarians who befriended the Poles and the Jews. The first messengers who went from Zablotow to Lemberg to the German command asked that the Hungarians be moved to Eastern Galicia where Vasil Evanski and his brother Ivan who, before the war was a film director at "OPAH" and understood Yiddish and Hebrew.

Because of the hatred of the Ukrainians towards the Jews, supplies of food were stopped and many families reached starvation. The Hungarian Army had made a small change and brought food by cars, which they sold, for gold, watches or other valuables. It did not bother them, at the same time, to take Jews daily to various forced labor and demand that the Jews pay ransom money for that food as a contribution to the Hungarian Army. A few Patrols attacked Jewish families searching for weapons and taking the opportunity to steal whatever they found.

A few German Nazis arrived in Kolomyja during the Hungarian Occupation and gathered about 200 Jews and moved them to Diatkavche near Kolomyja, where they were ordered to dig their own graves. During the work a Hungarian General happened to pass by, he opposed the German murderers, stopped the work and sent the Jews back to Kolomyja where they were released.

During the Hungarian occupation the police was mainly made up of Ukrainians who were previously Polish, then Russians, and now Ukrainian-German Patriots. They expressed their patriotism by arresting Moshe Lindaver, Shlomo Rosenbaum and the representative of the Soviet

Labor office and transported them to Petashnichin Concentration Camp, from which they did not return.

The Hungarian Army received its orders to leave the area in August and move further east. The control of our town was handed over to the Ukrainians Police and to a German Engineering Company who, together with the assistance of the local Jews, rebuilt the bridge over the Pruth River, and the Train Station. The Jews had to daily send approximately one hundred men to do that work. The German Authorities gave an order, with a firm warning of severe punishment, that all Jews must hand over their entire possessions of gold, Silver, Diamonds and other fine metal artifacts they had. Jews stood in long lines waiting their turn to hand over their important family Jewels. The Ukrainians for the administration, police and the German command took the best and nicest things they brought as well, for themselves.

The first order was just being carried out, when a new one arrived, with a death warning, that Jews were not allowed to leave the area. The intention was to make sure Jews would be killed, first by separating them from the rest of the population, and by preventing them from the opportunity to obtain food, and in this way, kill them. The field-gendarmes units, Shupa and the Gestapo carried out this order, they ordered the Yudenrat to send daily, at a certain time, all kinds of things which were unattainable, thus forcing the Yudenrat, not just once, to use the Internal Jewish police to take these things from the Jews themselves.

While they sucked the Jews' blood, by taking everything away from them, forcing them to hard labor, and starving them, the Gestapo officers were going around the different towns and planning the best methods to carry out the mass killings. They made detailed plans for each town including dates for the mass murder. The men in charge of the Kolomyja area were officer Falkman and his deputy, the Ukrainian Sematyuk from Ilintza, not far from Zablotow. Various unconfirmed rumors from Kolomyja and Stanislavov started arriving at the beginning of September 1941 about acts of mass murders. These acts were carried out in accordance with prepared name lists, first for the Jewish intelligence, and about attacks on Jews in Otinya, Nadvorna, Sniatin, and later in Kolomyja and Stanislavov, as well.

These rumors turned out to be true. The mass murder in Kosov that was held on October 16th and 17th, opened the eyes of all the Jews in the towns in the area, and made them realize that there was no intention of work camps, but simply for murder and killing. Firstly, each one made sure he had warm clothes, then they sewed some money into their clothes, to be able to buy from the hands of the murderers in the camp, or at least ease the trouble ahead.

Following the true news, which arrived in Zablotow about the action in Kosov and after the Yudenrat in Kolomyja, Horowitz and Yakov tried to lessen the severity of the incident. They visited the Jewish towns in the vicinity of Kolomyja to collect taxes, and at the same time calm the population calling these actions "nonsense", admitting it did happen to Jews but only once and it will not happen again. Everyone tried to run away from Zablotow the best way they could, according to his influence and opportunity, to a place where there had already been an action. Many Jews tried to reach Kosov to hide from the terrible storm, but only a small number managed to do so, while most of them were caught and arrested by the Ukrainian Police, stripped all their possessions, severely beaten and sent back to their homes. Death became obvious.

From mid October till December 22nd 1941 Zablotow's Jews scattered all over, to Gwazdietch, Klebichin, Raznavu, Kosov, and other places looking for 'so called' gentile friends, who took everything the Jews had and handed them over to the Treibers (Gestapo helpers). At best, they were simply expelled the next day, making it obvious that most of the Poles and the Ukrainians (except a few) gave Jews shelter for a short time, with the intention of robbing them and not as an act of human kindness.

During those days the Jewish apartments were virtually empty during the day, but at night they sneaked in from their hiding places to take what was left, and exchange them for potatoes, corn flour etc.

In this way the Jews managed to survive and keep their families informed about the possible date of the next act of mass murder of the Jews.

A few weeks before the mass murder, the murdering Nazis ordered three large pits to be dug on the side of the Chamau mountain making it clear they were for Anti-Aircraft guns. Jews who worked on the Pruth River bridge heard some rumors but could not definitely determine the intended use of the pits. The rumors were enough to cause great fear among the Jews and indescribable panic. Everyone ran away not knowing where or to whom, but just to get away from the place which smelled of forthcoming death. The terrible cold and hunger took the last bit of strength from the poor Jews. Gentiles, who were hiding Jews in their grain barns and sheds in exchange for gold or other expensive artifacts, forced them now to leave. This situation lasted for a long time, many Jews were forced to return to their apartments.

In every town the Gestapo organized a group of local Ukrainians (and Poles who wished to help) who at the time of the mass murder, when a signal was given, would get the Jews out of their hiding places and hand them over to the murdering Germans. In Zablotow they organized two such groups, one under the command of Von Kanihitski Von Balinitch , a specialist who obtained his education in the Hitler Youth Groups, and a son of a murderer of Jews (whom the Poles executed before the war). This group had the task of finding out where the Jews were going and where they were coming back from, and to assist in the murder Act. The second group was made up of Poles under the command of Tadash Kasawski and Frans the Chimney cleaner, who arrived from Kolomyja on the day of the murder. The whole Ukrainian police took part in this mass murder of the Jews under the command of Dicki.

When their spies informed the Gestapo that many Jews had returned to town they decided to have the murder Act on December 22nd 1941.

On that day, at 7:00 in the morning, a group of Gestapo Youth arrived from Kolomyja with their black wagons and waited in Demycze, which was a mixed suburb of the town where a few Jewish families lived among the Christians. They took all the Jews out of their homes and forced them to stand in rows in the City Square. Not a single Jewish home was spared in accordance with the detailed knowledge gathered by the local Hooligans, who marked their own homes with pictures of Christian Saints placed in the windows.

The first victim, who did not want to be led like a sheep to slaughter, was Boize Langshtein. He was shot on the spot. For the same transgression Yitzchak Singer, the son of Eliyahu, was shot and lost his hand. He was led together with all the rest to their execution. Another group of Jews, Chaim Tau Yakob's and Yisrael Ivanir among them, where taken out of the Kosov's Beit Hamidrash, still wearing their Talit and Tfilin.

The gathering was in the city's central square, from there they were sent in small groups to a wooden house, which had been previously emptied out. They had to hand over all their possessions and anyone caught was severely punished. While the Jews walked their last steps towards the three large pits on the Chamau Mountain, many Ukrainian gathered in the City Square and enjoyed watching the bloody "show". Their bloodthirstiness was so great that they even embittered their last minutes, throwing stones and pieces of metal at them. The Gestapo entered Mendel Toy's house yelling "Jews, get out!". In the first moments of confusion Mendel and his wife Henya tried to resist, citing their American Passports, and were immediately killed. During the march to the execution the German behaved in human way. Entering Dr. Nusenblat's house, the Gestapo found him studying scientific work in German, and all his Austrian medals from the First World War were lying on the table. They asked him where his wife and children were. He answered that they were visiting the neighbor. He was told to stay in the house, and they left. The Rabbi of Demycze, R' Avraham Hagger was hiding at the time and was able to escape the Action, however when he realized what was happening to all the Jews he decided his place was with all the others and he gave himself up to the murdering group. A similar incident happened to Moshe Fritz who was hiding with a group of Jews in the cellar of Sander Toy's house, when some gentiles informed the Gestapo about them. When the Gestapo came to the house they were afraid to go down to the cellar so they stayed outside and yelled, "Jews, get out!". Realizing the grave situation Moshe Fritz decided that since all the Jews were taken away, his life would have no meaning and he walked out accompanied by a few more Jews. Others, including Sander Toy stayed in the cellar, which saved them for a short time.

Twenty-nine Jews hid in Issac Yuren's cellar. An Ukrainian policeman, who was in the police force during the Soviet times, knew of the existence of a hidden door leading to a shoe storage room, now was looking for Jews hiding there, and handed them over to the Gestapo. Zelig Gross was among those twenty-nine, but he had miraculously escaped.

Many Jews who tried to escape were shot; not a single one was left hanging from posts. About one hundred were killed that day in town and were later buried in the Jewish cemetery. Zelig Schulman was the last one to be killed that day, when he got out of his hiding, thinking it was all over, a young Gestapo saw him and shot him.

About nine hundred Jews, men, women and children, were killed in this murderous act, and were buried in those three pits on Chamau Mountain. The pits were prepared a few weeks earlier especially for that purpose. The murderers left Zablotow singing the Nazi song. That same night the local Ukrainians ransacked the homes of the slaughtered Jews. In addition, the houses of the few who survived but were afraid to return to their houses were also ransacked. Kanihinski, who was in charge of the Gestapo, walked around in the Jewish neighborhood with his dog. When he spotted a Jew he released the hound to frighten the Jew and make sure he stayed away from his own home. Under great danger a few Jews managed to reenter their ransacked and ruined homes, and very few returned with their family. The Jews were frightened to death and moved around like shadows, from room to room, from neighbor to neighbor looking and asking for their parents, children, wives, relatives or acquaintances.

The cynical beastly manner in which the brown murderers behaved was so great that immediately following the Action they continued to persecute the Jews demanding, under a death threat, they hand over any clothing that had any piece of fur on it. For this purpose they organized Jewish committees which received orders to carry it out exactly to the letter. Naturally, the German and Ukrainian Gendarmes took for themselves and for their own wives the best and nicest furs. There was a short pause following this murderous act due probably to the cold winter, or because similar murderous actions had already taken place in all other Jewish towns in the vicinity, except in Kitau and Raznau. Following this short pause came the large scale desolation of the entire Polish Jewry under even worse conditions. During the pause, Jews prepared hiding places (bunkers) for themselves, and when a murdering German showed up in town they hid in their holes.

When the winter ended Jews felt their end was near. The already broken Jews received terrible rumors. It was rumored that the Yudenrat in Kolomyja received orders from the Gestapo to hand over all the children and elderly person who could not work to them. That meant killing their own parents, children, brothers and sisters. The Yudenrat refused the order. There were instances in Kolomyja where Jews were kidnapped by the Gestapo and traded for elderly or they were deported.

Everyday brought new and terrible reports. In one part of town a murdering act was carried out as follows; Jews were killed by gunfire, and then the house was set on fire forcing those who were hiding to come out or be burned alive. Jews in Gosditcher were concentrated on a few streets (Ghetto), and then a fire was set around them burning them alive without a way to escape.

On the seventh day of Passover 1942 the Gestapo entered the Jewish towns of Yablonov and Pistin on the road between Kolomyja and Kosov, and Kitow on the following day. They set fires from all sides killing the Jews in this terrible death. The streets were filled with Jewish corpses.

On the last day of Passover, in Zablotow, four hundred Jews were gathered and put in cattle wagons. Some of them suffocated in a short time in the wagons. No one knows where they were sent. In such inhumane conditions, the living envied the dead.

Following the last transport of Jews out of Zablotow, an order arrived to completely liquidate the entire Jewish population. With the exception of a few workers who were needed by the Germans, all Jews had to get to Kolomyja's Ghetto by the 24th of April 1942, where every one knew it would be a slow, but sure death. Each one was allowed to carry on his broken shoulders what ever he could, and march to Kolomyja. The twenty-kilometer march, with baggage, from Zablotow to Kolomyja was too much for these hungry Jews, in their state of mind.

Jews stood from morning till night in front of the offices of the Yudenrat in Zablotow, with their bags and belongings which had not yet been taken by their enemies, hoping that they could by some right stay in town as needed workers.

On the 24th of April all but 20 families walked to Kolomyja's ghetto. A horse and wagon was given for the sick and the elderly. Twenty people crowded into a single room. One kilogram bag of corn flour cost a dollar or more, if it was at all possible to obtain. Jews starved to death in the streets. Most of them could not even obtain potato skins. They bloated up from the hunger and died.

Two weeks later the Gestapo in Kolomyja organized various work-groups such as rag collectors, iron collectors, and farmers. Those who were included in these work-groups received some legitimacy and were able to return to their homes, thus creating small enclaves. Every Jew who still owned a few valuables tried to get into these work-groups to get a little legitimacy. While collecting the old rags and iron they had the opportunity to ask for some food and keep themselves and their family alive.

Jews suffered under these conditions until September 7th 1942 when all women and men with the work legitimacy, were required to register in Sniatin. They were brought into Sakal Hall, loaded into wagons and sent in various directions to their extermination. The rest of the Jews from Zablotow, who did not belong to the work-groups, were shipped as well.

Many suffocated in the wagons within an hour. Those who had more perseverance, especially the younger ones, realizing they had nothing to lose, started breaking the wagons and one after the other jumped out. Most of them were shot by the Gestapo Observation Group, which accompanied the transport and were stationed on the last wagon. Only very few managed to save their lives. The preferred place at that time was Chernovtsy where there were still left some Jews from the first Jewish expulsion of November 1941 to Transdenisterian. About twenty thousands lived there, in more or less good conditions.

The refugees in Chernovtsy did not have a roof over their head and were persecuted by the Rumanian police, many of them where deported and ended up back in the hands of Gestapo in Sniatin (on the Polish-Rumanian border).

Former Residents of Zablotow in the United States Build a Jewish School in the Old Home

Mr. Zondel Sheinhoren

During the first years of mass Jewish immigration to the United States, former residents from hundreds of cities and towns in Europe established separate organizations where all newcomers from those places were accepted as members.

These organizations got arranged to provide the new comers with material help and moral support. Each organization had its own financial account; a medical account providing free medicine; they're own Cemetery for departed members, and it provided small allowance for widows. During the first years these organizations were a great help to the newcomers as individuals and to the entire Jewish community in the United States.

In 1896-97 the Zabolotover Landsleit (Former residents of Zablotow) established the organization named " Our Zablotow's Rabbi Mendel Hager's organization for helping the sick". In 1899 when Mr. Yissachar Toy Z"L and Mr. Zundel Sheinhorn arrived in the United States there were 30 members in the organization. Today the organization holds 250 members and with wives and children under 18 there are about 700 people in the organization.

In 1918 immediately after the First World War the organizations established what was called Relief Committees, that collected money amongst their members in order to help the needy in their old hometowns. Naturally, the Zablotowers did the same thing.

In a short time we collected 3,000 dollars and later further 2,000 dollars which were sent to Zablotow and distributed to the needy.

Most of the residents in Zablotow were convinced that we did our duty, but a few of us still felt that "man can not live on bread alone" and what was really required was to establish something spiritual and cultural.

The local Zablotowers formed a special group with the specific goal to do something in this regard.

They were: Yissachar Toy, Zundel Sheinhorn, Yakov Sheinhorn, Moshe Hertzog (son-in-law of Shmuel Tilinger), Aaron Straus, Zeide Altman, Shlomo Yoseph Shtadler, Moshe Shaffer, Avramche Oyerbach, Moshe Hirsch (son-in-law of Litman Reiter), Moshe Shtadler and Max Shtadler. We decided to build and to maintain a modern Jewish school in Zablotow with room for culture and social activities.

When it was decided to do the above, we called upon a few learned Zionist of Zablotow. They were Natan Karen, Mordechai Karen, Ben-Zion Toy and Zelig Gross, the son of the slaughterer David Hersh, and asked them to tell us their opinion about the plan and how much money would be required for it.

Everyone in Zablotow accepted the plan. The ongoing expenses were estimated to be about $60 a month which we must send over. This is in addition to the money the American group must send for the local needy residents of Zablotow and for those returning after the war. Today's residents of Zablotow on the other hand wished to pay for the expenses of the place and for the teacher and the maintenance man by themselves.

We immediately accepted that proposal and sent money for the construction. They immediately rented a place, hired a teacher and opened the school. From our end, we sent them precisely each month the above mentioned 60 Dollars besides extra money to cover unforeseen expenses, and the school made good progress.

After two years the school's management notified us that the place was too small, they need a second teacher as well, since the number of children had increased. They suggested we purchase for this purpose, the house of Evilishen Dexer Litch for 4, 000 Dollars. A thousand Dollars they were willing to donate, while we would give 3,000 Dollars and add 20 Dollars to the monthly donation to cover the expense of the second teacher.

After giving it some thought we decided to transfer the whole matter to Dr. Alexander Reiterman, a cousin of Yissachar Toy, who was a prominent lawyer, and at that time the President of the Jewish Community in Stanislavov and leader of the Polish Zionists.

Dr. Reiterman visited Zablotow, checked the matter and sent us a positive report. He promised us that should we buy the house to enlarge the school, he would oversee the entire operation of the institute, the studies and the building to ensure proper operation of the school.

We sent the money and he purchased the house. Due to Polish Laws, which did not allow outsiders to buy land in Poland, Dr. Reiterman presented Yissachar Toy as the buyer of the house and gave him a receipt for 3,000 Dollars.

They moved into the new location enlarging the school and added another teacher. Since that time we sent 80 Dollars each month besides the cost of basic necessities and other expenses totaling about 100 Dollars a month.

During the first 3-4 years the school operated nicely and was a great success. Later although management was not as before, the school still operated more or less as expected of them. As we had set forth, namely to keep the Jewish children off the streets, to provide them with basic Jewish and general knowledge, and to provide the older youth a place where to hold their Zionist and cultural meetings.

The school existed and functioned the entire time till the outbreak of the Second World War.

This is more or less the history of the Jewish school in Zablotow. It is possible that I have not mentioned some details exactly, but I can promise that the main facts and figures are exact and correct.

Conclusion

Duplicate of Hebrew Introduction section, but in Yiddish.

Index of Surnames, Towns, Professions, and Miscellaneous

This section contains an index created from the body of the Yizkor Book. Included in the index are surnames, town names, and other unique names. The page numbers refer to the page numbers in the original Yizkor Book.

(These pages are page numbers of the Original Yizkor Book, not the page numbers of this translation)

Blima, 56

Bloch, 20, 21, 32

Blushtein, 19, 20

Bnei-Brak, 41

Bohorodshani, 34

Boimel, 16

Bomes, 22

Borodshin, 68

Borohotshani, 23

Botshatsh, 64

Brotherstavo, 83

Buber, 80

Bukovina, 3, 4, 8, 9, 15, 19, 20, 25, 27, 28, 29, 30, 31, 32, 37, 38, 40, 42, 44, 45, 47, 51, 52, 53, 57, 61, 67, 69

Butchers, 59

Butschki, 9

C

Carpenters, 56

Carters, 57, 58

Chalibitchin, 64

Chalibitchner, 62

Chalutz, 34

Chamau, 95, 96, 97

Chamdrool, 12

Charab, 32

Chatam Soffer, 42

Chavtan, 39

Chayot, 26

Chazan, 6, 8, 13, 14, 16, 20, 21, 22, 25, 26, 30, 31, 32, 36, 38, 42, 50, 54

Chazan Yeshayahu, 48

Cheder, 12, 19, 32, 37, 43, 50, 54

Cheders, 26, 29, 32, 37, 46, 49, 51, 53

Ill'intse, 35, 36, 62, 87

Ilintza, 94

Ish-Shalom, 67

Ita, 41, 42

Itzik, 27, 48, 49

Ivanir, 96

Izy, 55, 88

J

Judges, 18, 33, 61

K

Kabala, 64

Kahane, 42, 43

Kalir, 18, 60

Kalush, 7, 62

Kanihinski, 97

Kanihitski, 96

Karmes, 12

Karpathian Mountains, 19, 25, 28, 38, 48, 51, 52, 80

Karschivaski, 72

Karsel, 1, 2, 3, 13, 14, 16, 53, 60, 61, 66, 75, 79

Kasawski, 96

Kashrut, 69

Keis, 41

Keish, 1, 2, 3, 4, 11, 12, 22, 26, 27, 35, 39, 40, 42, 44, 92

Kelbali, 56

Kelikhov, 87

Keren, 39

Kersel, 14

Kitau, 97

Kitow, 98

Kiydantse, 8

Index of Surnames

This section contains an index created from the body of this translation of the Yizkor Book.

These pages are page numbers of this translation of the Yizkor Book.

Laker, 18, 136
Landau, 34, 53
Langshtein, 119, 136
Lebel, 31, 136
Leib, 7, 17, 18
Leibel, 19, 20, 22, 26, 136
Lester, 67
Leviner, 40, 81, 137
Libber, 61, 74, 82
Libs, 81
Lichtenshtein, 51, 137
Lindaver, 116, 137
Lindbaum, 53, 137
Linder, 29, 137
Litch, 124, 137
Locker, 28, 31, 137

M

Maher, 22, 39, 137
Maibaum, 87, 137
Maltchek, 72, 137
Manches, 54, 137
Manis, 73, 137
Meir'el, 7, 137
Melamed, 25, 137
Meltzer, 27, 29, 30, 31, 49, 53, 80, 81, 137
Mendel, 7
Mher, 3, 137
Milich, 66, 138
Miller, 19, 32, 138
Mimlis, 46, 60, 138
Mintzer, 26, 138
Moderin, 51, 138

N

Neinberg, 74, 138
Nusberg, 25, 138
Nusenblat, 106, 109, 111, 119, 138

O

Oierbach, 20, 138
Orenshtein, 19, 41, 138
Oslover, 75, 139
Oyerbach, 25, 41, 65, 72, 124, 139

P

Parless, 84, 139
Pasternak, 40, 139
Perel's, 19
Peretz, 34, 36, 53, 139
Periliss, 75, 139

Pessi-Leah, 7
Pistiner, 57, 139
Potelinski, 71, 139
Preminger, 32, 140
Pupik, 75, 140

Q

Queen Maria Teresa, 57

R

Rabbi Avraham, 10
Rabbi Chaim, 9
Rabbi Damta, 110
Rabbi David, 8, 13
Rabbi Gershon, 8
Rabbi Itchele, 82
Rabbi Mendele, 8, 10, 12, 59
Rabbi Moshe, 8, 9
Rabbi of Tysmenitsa, 8
Rabbi Shalom, 13
Rabbi Yankele, 8, 59
Rabbi Yenkele, 65
Radish, 107
Rata, 11, 36, 37, 52, 140
Reiber, 22
Reisenberg, 77, 140
Reisher, 60, 65, 111, 140
Reiter, 37, 70, 74, 124, 140
Reiterman, 124, 140
Reizel, 9, 25, 140
Resher, 65, 140
Ridniker, 38, 140
Riterman, 43, 140
Rokach, 13, 140
Rosenbaum, 25, 116, 140
Rosenboim, 17, 25, 34, 42, 43, 44, 65, 67, 73, 99, 140
Rosenhak, 91, 140
Rosenshtock, 54, 141
Rosenshtroich, 31, 141
Rosenthal, 19, 53, 141
Rotfeld, 59, 141
Roysner, 28, 141
Rubin, 18, 20, 21, 22, 26, 36, 38, 48, 55, 58, 66, 80, 93, 106, 108, 141

S

Salpeter, 10, 12, 14, 25, 54, 141
Salts, 3, 141
Schulman, 120
Sematyuk, 117, 141
Shafer, 26, 29, 74, 141